FOR THE SAKE OF ME US

A MARRIAGE PREPARATION WORKBOOK

JEROME & KORRIE PAYNE

www.TrueVinePublishing.org

"FOR THE SAKE OF US"
A Marriage Preparation Workbook 2nd Print
Jerome and Korrie Payne

Published by True Vine Publishing Co. LLC
810 Dominican Dr. Ste. 103
Nashville, TN 37228
www.TrueVinePublishing.org

ISBN: 978-1-956469-48-6 Paperback
ISBN: 978-1-956469-40-0 eBook

Printed in the United States —Second Printing
Email: jpministries@jpministries.net

ACKNOWLEDGMENTS:

A Big thanks to those couples that participated in the marriage focus group. Your experience and insight was invaluable. Also, other thanks are in order for those couples that provided testimonials that you will read at the end of some of the chapters. I appreciate their open and honest sharing; hopefully their testimonials will give you greater insight into the marriage relationship. To my beautiful wife Korrie, It has been a blast sharing this marriage journey with you. My love for you grow deeper each day. I am also grateful for your dedication, wisdom, and input into this project. To our three daughters, Kristen, Kennedy, Karrington thanks for your support and unsolicited feedback.

Special thanks to the amazing couples who provided testimonials and videos.

TABLE OF CONTENTS:

By accepting counseling from J.P. Ministries, I

(Print Name) _____

Agree to and understand the following: (Please initial each)

_____ The counseling provided by JPM is faith-based and spiritual in nature.

_____ The content of your session are completely confidential except where limited by law. These limitations include any plan to harm others or self along with issues of child and/or elder abuse.

_____ The counseling received from JPM is not based on secular psychology or psychiatric, nor are the counselors licensed as psychotherapists or mental health professionals.

_____ Waiver of liability: In consideration for receiving any form of counseling from JPM, the person receiving the counseling agrees to release and waive any and all claims of any kind against the ministry, the staff, the counselors, which may arise from result out of, or be related to conduct or advice given.

I have carefully read this information sheet and agree to all of the state terms and conditions.

Signature: _____

Date:_____

PREPARING COUPLES FOR MARRIAGE

Name: _____

Address: _____

_____

Phone: Cell _____ email:_____

DOB _____   Age _____

Are you saved Yes ___ No ___ If yes, how long?_____

Married before: Yes _____ No _____

Were you friends before dating: Yes ____ No ____
If yes, how long? _____

Length of time for dating: _____

 Are you currently engaged: Yes _____ No _____
If yes, how long? _____

Wedding date/ time:_____

Wedding Location _____

Wedding Rehearsal Date: _____
Size of wedding party   _____
Who is officiating the Ceremony _____

S.W.O.T ANALYSIS

Strengths: (Please list what you consider to be the strengths in your relationship

_____

_____

_____

_____

Weaknesses: (Please list the weaknesses you have seen or think may be in the relationship)

_____

_____

_____

_____

Opportunities: (Please list areas where improvements can be made in the relationship)

_____

_____

_____

_____

Threats: (please list the things, people or actions that propose a threat to your marriage– also what do you see as potential threats)

_____

_____

_____

_____

ABSTINENCE OF SEX

Barry and Cathy
Married 34 Years

1 Corinthians 6:12-20 (NIV)
Sexual Immorality

"I have the right to do anything" you say—but not everything is beneficial. "I have the right to do anything" – but I will not be mastered by anything. You say, "Food is for the stomach and the stomach for food, and God will destroy them both." The body, however, is not meant for sexual immorality but for the Lord, and the Lord for the body. By his power God raised the Lord from the dead, and he will raise us also. Do you not know that your bodies are members of Christ himself? Shall I then take the members of Christ and unite them with a prostitute? Never! Do you not know that he who unites himself with a prostitute is one with her in body? For it is said, "The two will become one flesh." But whoever is united with the Lord is one with him in spirit.

Flee from sexual immorality. All other sins a person commits are outside the body, but whoever sins sexually, sins against their own body. Do you not know that your bodies are temples of the Holy Spirit, who is in you, whom you have received from God? You are not your own, you were bought at a price. Therefore honor God with your bodies.

If you have not abstained from sexual acts, we asked that you do so while learning to build a long-lasting relationship. We also recommend that you ask God for forgiveness and remain abstinent until you are married. If you make this commitment, you will see God's hand on your marriage and the experience will be well worth it.

INTRODUCTION:

Marriage is so full of adventure and excitement! How you ask? It's so adventurous in ways unimaginable. For instance, at times, you never know what to expect! So many times we make plans for our future, and seldom do we think about detours along the way. When a detour is needed, you and your mate will think about options and ideas that were never thought of before. That's the adventure of two souls uniting as one to navigate the hurdles of life.

Just having someone there who truly cares for you and want to be with you for the rest of your life is exciting! Wanting to please each other through being a friend, confidant and lover is amazing! The author of marriage, our Lord and Savior Jesus Christ, designed and created marriage the same way he designed and created us! To be exciting and adventurous!

He has a plan to make your marriage successful! The reason a manual comes with everything that we purchase is so we'll always have it when we need to fix, or remind ourselves how the equipment works. The bible does that exact same thing.It teaches how we should love each other; forgive each other, and how to respect each other. "For the Sake of me Us" is exactly what the bible teaches, a tool that's designed to eliminate as many surprises as possible as you learn about yourself and your partner. May God bless your marriage journey.

-Korrie Payne

THE RIGHT FOUNDATION FOR MARRIAGE:

Pastor Bruce & Lady Evon
Married 49 Years

Bishop Horace and Pastor Kiwanis
Married 50 Years

THE MARRIAGE JOURNEY:

You are about to embark on one of the greatest journeys of your life; the marriage journey.

The excitement and enjoyment that you receive will be in direct proportion to what you give.

This journey requires you to give unselfishly, share openly, and love unconditionally.

QUESTIONS FOR YOU:

- What is your definition of marriage?
- Why is this the right time for marriage?
- Why do you want to get married?
- What do you want out of marriage?

Review the following statements below. If you agree, check the agree box. If you disagree, check the disagree box.

o Agree-
o Disagree   Marriage is a lifelong commitment

o Agree
o Disagree   One aspect of marriage is to refine our character

o Agree
o Disagree   Marriage is God's idea

o Agree
o Disagree   Marriage is easy, and does not require work

o Agree
o Disagree   Marriage will change my partners bad habits

Infatuation:

There are some feelings we have when infatuated, that can be confused with love. Infatuation normally occurs early in a relationship, and you feel as if this could be the person you spend the rest of your life with.

Look over the statements below. Circle the option that correspond to your behavior toward your future spouse:

- **You are consumed with thinking of him or her**
  Never   Occasionally   Sometimes   Often   Regularly

- **You do silly or risky actions to be together**
  Never   Occasionally   Sometimes   Often   Regularly

- **You are blind to his or her faults**
  Never   Occasionally   Sometimes   Often   Regularly

- **You give up your own personality or morals for his or her affection**
  Never   Occasionally   Sometimes   Often   Regularly

- **You are consumed with being noticed by him or her**
  Never   Occasionally   Sometimes   Often   Regularly

- **You often spend quality time together**
  Never   Occasionally   Sometimes   Often   Regularly

Infatuation is a temporary condition, and should not be used as a sign to pursue a relationship

What is Love?

Often times in the English language we use the word love in a thousand insignificant ways. As a matter of fact, we assign so many meanings to the word love that it ceases to mean much of anything. We use it to express any trivial desire or attraction. This uncertain definition of love can make it difficult to discern its proper place in a marriage relationship.

The Greek language is much more precise than the English in describing relationships. From this language, the Bible gives us three words (Eros, Phileo, and Agape) that can be translated into English as "love." All three should be present in a nurturing marriage.

The Language of Love:

Eros: Is a need centered love or desire based on attraction and fulfillment. **Eros** is characterized by passion and sexual desire. The English word "erotic" is borrowed from this word. This **Eros** aspect of love is God given and necessary for marriages to succeed; however, marriage cannot be sustained by **Eros** alone. It's part of God's plan, but not all of it.

Phileo: Is a friendship love. The Bible uses the word "companionship" several times to describe this part of a marriage. **Phileo** love means reciprocal sharing of time, hobbies, activities, home, games, and other aspects of fellowship. **Phileo** is that mutuality and friendship part of love. It is the love that makes husband and wives best friends.

Agape: This is the supreme love, a giving love. **Agape** reaches out even if the person being loved doesn't deserve or recognize the love. **Agape** is a selfless, unconditional, divine, and self-sacrificing love.

For the next several questions, please choose a number from 1-10 and write it next to each statement to indicate how much you agree with that statement:

1	2	3	4	5	6	7	8	9	10
Disagree		Somewhat Disagree		Somewhat agree		Agree		Strongly agree	

1. _____ Friendship is important for a marriage to survive
2. _____ My future spouse and I started out as friends
3. _____ My partner and I enjoy spending time together
4. _____ I feel my spouse has unconditional love for me
5. _____ I have witness unselfish acts of love from my partner
6. _____ After we are married, I expect passion and sexual desire to play an important part in our marriage
7. _____ Passion and sexual desire is the only element we will need in our marriage

The Characteristics of Love:

1st Corinthians 13; is known as the love chapter in the Bible. It clearly outlines the characteristics of true love, and characteristics that prevent true love. (Please take time to review this chapter) Knowing and displaying the right characteristics, while avoiding the ones that prevent true love, are vital to the survival of any marriage. You will find a list of some of these traits from this chapter below: Let's examine how prevalent they are in your relationship.

Look at the characteristics below and use this scale to categorize how much each one is displayed in your relationship.

Rate your level of exhibiting these characteristics (column 1 under "you") then rate your future spouse level of exhibiting these characteristics (column 2 under "spouse").

You will use the third column shortly.

1. Not Present 2. Sometimes Present 3. Present 4. Often Present 5. Regularly Present

As an example- a (1) indicates the characteristics are not present at all. While a (5) indicates the characteristics are regularly present.

Good Traits:

	YOU	SPOUSE	Difference
Patience	____	____	____
Kindness	____	____	____
Trust	____	____	____
Always Hope	____	____	____
Loves Truth	____	____	____
Always Trust	____	____	____

Bad Traits:

Easily Angered   ___   ___   ___

13 Jealous   ___   ___   ___

Proud   ___   ___   ___

Rude   ___   ___   ___

Boastful   ___   ___   ___

Now you and your partner should compare your list, and put a check in column 3 (difference) for any characteristics where you have a significant scoring difference. These are the areas you should spend time discussing.

Love in Action:

• Describe the love you have for your partner

_____
_____
_____
_____

• Describe your willingness to put your partner's happiness before your own

_____
_____
_____
_____

• How do you know this love will last a lifetime

_____
_____
_____
_____

- In one word, describe what a great marriage needs (do not use the word love)

_____

_____

_____

_____

- Why do you believe this is the right person to marry? Do you know this love will last a lifetime?

_____

_____

_____

_____

- Do you love this person with all your heart, and no longer feel the urge to search for someone else?

_____

_____

_____

_____

The Perfect Model:

Christ displayed the ultimate act of love by dying for us while we were still sinners and completely unworthy. God designed marriage as a place to witness this unparalleled act of unconditional love first hand. Christ and His relationship to the church is the perfect model of marriage.

Marriage Harmony:

Now let's look at the roles and responsibilities God gave husbands and wives. This information can be found in Ephesians 5:21-33. After each statement, please write your interpretation of its meaning:

Submit to one another out of reverence for Christ, Ephesians 5:21

_____

_____

_____

_____

Wives, submit to your husbands as to the Lord. For the husband is the head of the wife as Christ is the head of the church. His body, of which he is the savior. Now as the church submits to Christ, so also wives should submit to their husbands in everything. (Ephesians 5:22-24)

_____

_____

_____

_____

Husbands love your wives, just as Christ loved the church and gave himself up for her. To make her holy, cleansing her by the washing with water through the word, and to present her to himself as a radiant church, without stain or wrinkle or any other blemish, but holy and blameless. In this same way, husbands ought to love their wives as their own bodies. He who loves his wife loves himself. After all, no one ever hated his own body, but he feeds and cares for it, just as Christ does the church. For we are members of his body. For this reason a man will leave his father and mother and be united to his wife, and the two will become one flesh. This is a profound mystery- but I am talking about Christ and the church. However, each one of you must love his wife as he loves himself, and the wife must respect her husband. (Ephesians 5:25-33)

_____

_____

_____

_____

Four Purposes: Below are four of the purposes that the bible list for marriages:

- Companionship - It was not good that man be alone, so God made him a helper. (Genesis 2:18)

- Procreation - Be fruitful and multiply. Raise up children to serve God. (Genesis 1:28) 16

- Pleasure - God has given marriage where we can enjoy physical relations without guilt - Hebrews 13:4

- Illustration - Christ relationship to the church - Ephesians 5:25

More Discussions:

History-

1. Describe the relationship between your father and mother.

_____
_____
_____
_____

2. Describe the married relationship you observed in the household where you grew-up.

_____
_____
_____
_____

3. What healthy images of marriage were you exposed to growing up?

_____
_____
_____
_____

4. How was love expressed in your home when you were growing up?

_____
_____
_____
_____

5. Did you feel secure as a child? Explain;

_____
_____
_____
_____

Important Questions

1. Do you love this person so much that you are willing to lay down your life for him or her?

   _____

   _____

   _____

   _____

2. Have you ever lived independently and supported yourself for at least a year?

   _____

   _____

   _____

   _____

3. Do most people consider you emotionally mature, able to compromise, share your feelings, and handle anger constructively?

   _____

   _____

   _____

   _____

4. Are you able to keep commitments and delay gratification?

   _____

   _____

   _____

   _____

5. Do you feel you have a good understanding of your weaknesses? List them below:

   _____

   _____

   _____

   _____

6. Do you and your future spouse share common goals, beliefs, and values?

_____
_____
_____
_____

7. Have you both prayed individually about getting married?

_____
_____
_____
_____

8. What have you shared with your mate about your past relationships?

_____
_____
_____
_____

9. What do you know about your future mate's:
   a) Credit history
   b) Relationship history
   c) Employment history
   d) Health history

_____
_____
_____
_____

10. Have you accepted Christ as your Lord and Savior?

_____
_____
_____
_____

STAYING TOGETHER

Brian and Rachel
Married 20 Years

THE FAITH JOURNEY

BEING EQUALLY YOKED

Alex and Adreena
Married 13 Years

OUR FAITH WALK TOGETHER

In 2 Corinthians 6:14, the Apostle Paul says that believers should not "be unequally yoked with non-believers." We know this passage refers to being bound in a relationship with another person. No relationship is more binding than marriage.

This passage has the Old Testament command in view (Deuteronomy 22:10). "You shall not plow with and ox and a donkey together."

These two animals are of a very different size and strength. The ox is much stronger, and will pull in a different manner. The donkey would be forced to work extra hard, just to keep up and not be strangled.

Paul's principle is clear; a believer must not marry an unbeliever. When two believers are married, they are commonly dedicated to the lordship of Christ. They have a shared faith to find answers to the questions and problems of life. In contrast, when a believer marries an unbeliever they lack this mutuality of faith and commitment. Issues of contrasting beliefs will certainly be a problem. The both of you can be believers and have a difference of opinion about some of the non-important issues of the Christian faith. But, there should be an agreement as to who Jesus is and the basic tenets of the Christian faith.

Now, both of you should complete the questions below: to share details about your faith.

History:

- Did you grow up in the Christian faith?

_____

_____

_____

_____

- Describe your spiritual life as a teen?

_____

_____

_____

_____

- What did your parents teach you about God, Jesus, and the Bible?

_____
_____
_____
_____

- Did you read the bible as a teen? If so, how often?

_____
_____
_____
_____

- Were there any events that impacted your faith negatively as a teen?

_____
_____
_____
_____

More Discussion:

- Have you accepted Christ as your Lord and Savior?

_____
_____
_____
_____

- Who is God to you?

_____
_____
_____
_____

- Are you a member of a church?

_____
_____
_____
_____

- Do you value weekly worship

_____

_____

_____

_____

- What code of ethics guide your life

_____

_____

_____

_____

- Describe your current relationship with God.

_____

_____

_____

_____

- Explain the first time you recognized God's hand in your life?

_____

_____

_____

_____

- How important is your faith to you?

_____

_____

_____

_____

- Do you prefer one denomination over another?

_____

_____

_____

_____

- What has been the extent of your church involvement?

_____

_____

_____

_____

- How often do you read or study the bible?

_____

_____

_____

_____

- How often do you pray? What do you pray about?

_____

_____

_____

_____

- Have you been baptized

_____

_____

_____

_____

- Describe your personal relationship with Jesus.

_____

_____

_____

_____

- What is your view on eternal life?

_____

_____

_____

_____

- What is your view on heaven?

_____

_____

_____

_____

> **Review the questions below: If you agree with the statement check "YES", if you disagree, check "NO".**

	YES	NO
1. Does absolute moral truth exist?	O	O
2. Is absolute truth defined by the bible?	O	O
3. Did Jesus Christ live a sinless life?	O	O
4. Is salvation a free gift from God?	O	O
5. Is Satan real?	O	O

4 ATTACHMENT STYLES

Eddie and Melissa
Married 21 Years

WHAT IS ATTACHMENT?

Attachment, or the attachment bond, is the emotional connection you formed as an infant with your primary caregiver–probably your mother. The quality of the bonding you experienced during this first relationship often determines how well you relate to other people and respond to intimacy throughout life.

If your primary caretaker made you feel safe and understood as an infant, if they were able to respond to your cries and accurately interpret your changing physical and emotional needs, then you likely developed a successful, secure attachment. As an adult, that usually translates to being self-confident, trusting, and hopeful, with an ability to heavily manage conflict, respond to intimacy, and navigate the ups and downs of romantic relationships.

If you experience confusing, frightening, or inconsistent emotional communication during infancy, though, if your caregiver was unable to consistently comfort you or respond to your needs, you're more likely to have experienced an unsuccessful or insecure attachment. Infants with insecure attachment often grow into adults who have difficulty understanding their own emotions and feelings of others, limiting their ability to build or maintain stable relationships. They may find it difficult to quick connect to others, share way from intimacy, or be too clingy, fearful, or anxious in a relationship.

Secure Attachment Style:

Empathetic and able to set appropriate boundaries, people with secure attachment tend to feel safe, stable, and more satisfied in their close relationships. While they don't fear being on their own, they usually thrive in coles, meaningful relationships. Having a secure attachment style doesn't mean you're perfect or you don't experience relationship problems. But you liely feel secure enough to take responsibility for your own mistake and failings, and are willing to seek help and support when you need it.

- You appreciate your own self-worth and you're able to be yourself in an intimate relationship. You're comfortable expressing your feelings, hopes, and needs.

- You find satisfaction in being with outhers, openly seek support and comfort from your partner, but don't get lovely anxious when the two of you are apart.

- You're similarly happy for your partner to rely on you for support.

- You're able to maintain your emotional balance and seek healthy ways to manage confict in a close relationship.

- When faced with disappointment, setbacks, and misfortune in your relationships as well as other parts of your life, you're resilient enough to bounce back.

DISORGANIZED/ DISORIENTED ATTACHMENT STYLE

Disorganized/disoriented attachment, also referred to as fearful-avoidant attachment, stems from intense fear, often as a result of childhood trauma, neglect, or abuse. Adults with this style of insecure attachment tend to feel they don't deserve love or closeness in a relationship.

If you have a disorganized attachment style, you've likely never learned to self-sooth your emotions, so both relationships and the world around you can feel frightening and unsafe. If you experienced abuse as a child, you may try to replicate the same abusive patterns of behavior as an adult.

- You probably find intimate relationships confusing and unsettling, often swinging between emotional extremes of love and hate for a partner.

- You may be insensitive towards your partner, selfish, controlling, and untrusting, which can lead to explosive or even abusive behavior. And you can be just as hard on yourself as you are on others.

- You may exhibit antisocial or negative behavior patters, abuse alcohol or drugs, or prone to aggression or violence.

- Others may despair at your refusal to take responsibility for your actions.

- While you crave the security and safety of a meaningful, intimate relationship, you also feel unworth of love and terrified of getting hurt again.

- Your childhood may have been shaped by abuse, neglect, or trauma.

ANXIOUS ATTACHMENT STYLE

People with an anxious attachment style tend to be overly needy. As the labels suggest, people with this attachment style are often anxious and uncertain, lacking in self-esteem. They crave emotional intimacy but worry that others don't want to be with them.

If you have an anxious attachment style, you may be embarrassed about being too clingy or your constant need for love and attention. Or you may feel worn down by fear and anxiety about whether your partner really loves you.

- You want to be in a relationship and crave feelings of closeness and intimacy with a significant other, but you struggle to feel that you can trust or fully rely on your partner.

- Being in an intimate relationship tends to take over your life and you become overly fixated on the other person.

- You may find it difficult to observe boundaries, viewing space between you as a threat, something that can provoke panic, anger, or fear that your partner no longer wants you.

- A lot of your sense of self-wroth rests on how you feel you're being treatted in the relationship and you tend to overreact to any perceived threats to the relationship.

- You feel anxious or jealous when away from your partner and may use guilt, controlling behavior, or other manipulative tactics to keep them close.

- You need constant reassurance and lots of attention from your partner.

AVOIDANT-DISMISSIVE ATTACHMENT STYLE

Adults with an avoidant-dismissive insecure attachment style are the opposite of those who are ambivalent or anxious-preoccupied. Instead of craving intimacy, they're so wary of closeness they try to avoid emotional connection with others. They'd rather not rely on others, or have others rely on them.

As someone with an avoidant-dismissive attachment style, you tend to find it difficult to tolerate emotionally intimacy. You value your independence and freedom to the point where you can feel uncomfortable with, even stifled by, intimacy and closeness in a romantic relationship.

- You're an independent person, content to care for yourself and don't feel you need others.

- The more someone tries to get close to you or the needier a partner becomes, the more you tend to withdraw.

- You're uncomfortable with your emotions and partners often accuse you of being distant and closed off, rigid and intolerant. In return, you accuse them of being too needy.

- You're prone to minimize or disregard your partner's feelings, keep secrets from them, engage in affairs, and even end relationships in order to regain your sense of freedom.

- You may prefer fleeting, casual relationships to long-term intimate ones, or you seek out partners who are equally independent, ones who'll keep their distance emotionally.

ATTACHMENT STYLES:

Circle the best answer below:

1. I shouldn't have to read your mind.
    A. Secure
    B. Anxious
    C. Disorganized/ Disoriented
    D. Avoidant-Dismissive

2. I'm confident in who I am, also sensitive to the relationship.
    A. Avoidant-Dismissive
    B. Anxious
    C. Secure
    D. Disorganized/Disoriented

3. I need my space and don't want to be bothered.
    A. Anxious
    B. Avoidant-Dismissive
    C. Secure
    D. Disorganized/Disoriented

4. I need to check your phone daily to make sure there's no cheating.
    A. Disorganized/ Disoriented
    B. Anxious
    C. Avoidant-Dismissive
    D. Secure

5. I don't need affection and you shouldn't either!
    A. Secure
    B. Anxious
    C. Disorganized/Disoriented
    D. Avoidant-Dismissive

6. Whatever we face, we will get through it.
    A. Secure
    B. Avoidant-Dismissive
    C. Anxious
    D. Disorganized/Disoriented

7. I will tell everybody you know if you leave me!
    A. Avoidant-Dismissive
    B. Disorganized/Disoriented
    C. Anxious
    D. Secure

8. I need you to tell and show me how much you love me 4 times a day.
   A. Anxious
   B. Secure
   C. Avoidant-Dismissive
   D. Disorganized/Disoriented

THE POWER OF FORGIVENESS

Denai and Tanisha
Married 12 Years

THE POWER OF FORGIVENESS:

Forgiveness of Others:

Providing someone forgiveness that you believe wronged or hurt you, can be a very difficult thing to do. As a matter of fact, some people live their entire lives unwilling to forgive someone that has hurt them. Often times the refusal of forgiveness is seen as a type of power they hold over that person. Somehow, they think this will provide a way for revenge or cause this person to feel the pain they have created. The wounds can run deep and leave lasting feelings of anger, bitterness, and resentment, making it more difficult to see how the power of forgiveness can release them from their prison of pain.

Forgiveness of Oneself:

Another important element of forgiveness is the thought one must forgive oneself. The feelings of anger, bitterness, and resentment may not have been caused by someone else. But could be an internal battle you are having due to bad decisions, or mistakes. You may have a constant, critical voice in your head reminding you of your past, or the pain you may have caused others. Perhaps you feel you could get past this pain if you could just forgive yourself.

The notion of "forgiving oneself" is a popular one today. Psychologists tell us we must forgive ourselves for whatever wrong we may have done in the past. However, scripture says absolutely nothing about forgiving oneself. There is not one word, verse, or even a description of anybody coming to terms with the pain in his or her own life by forgiving him or herself. The bible speaks of vertical forgiveness (God forgiving a person), and horizontal forgiveness (one person forgiving another).

This concept of "self-forgiveness" is absent from the bible because if you are a believer; repent of your sins, and take them before the Lord, then you are forgiven. (1 John 1:9) You must accept by faith this grace of God, granted through the finished work of Christ on the cross. God's forgiveness is total and complete within itself, and you only need to accept it.

<u>Question for You:</u>

- Please give your definition of forgiveness.

_____
_____
_____
_____

- How important is forgiveness in a marriage?

_____
_____
_____
_____

- How do you normally respond when you are offended?

_____
_____
_____
_____

- How does your partner respond when they are offended?

_____
_____
_____
_____

What is Forgiveness?

A. Choice- A choice we make through a decision of our will, it is not based on emotions
B. Command- The bible commands us to forgive others as God has forgiven us {Matthew 6:14-16}
C. Event- The event is when you make the decision to forgive
D. Process- The time it takes for the healing process to occur. When you say "I forgive you" the hurt and pain does not just leave suddenly, it takes time for you to completely heal from the hurt.

Your Accountability:

Your accountability is the willingness to forgive. As you act in obedience to God, He will give you comfort and help through the healing process. He is the God of all comfort. Put your focus on God during this process, and allow Him to strengthen your heart. Trust Him to enact justice according to His will.

- Is there someone that offended you, which you have not forgiven? Explain;

_____

_____

_____

_____

- Do you feel the bible command us to forgive?

_____

_____

_____

_____

- List a time in the past when you forgave someone of an offense against you.

_____

_____

_____

_____

- Should you forgive when you don't feel like it?

_____

_____

_____

_____

What Forgiveness is Not:

• Letting Offender Go—Forgiveness doesn't mean you deny the person's responsibility for hurting you, or justify the wrong. You can forgive the person without excusing their actions.
• Forgetting - You are not going to forget, but you can chose not to remember or bring it up
• Revenge - You must remove all feelings of getting even. And trust God to take care of justice
• Mending Relationship - Just because you forgive someone does not mean the relationship will return to a happy place. The relationship may never be reconciled
• A Feeling - You can't wait until you feel like forgiving someone, but rather; forgiveness is a choice we make

• What are your thoughts and feelings about revenge?

_____

_____

_____

_____

• How do you feel when you have to forgive someone that offended you, when they do not say they're sorry?

_____

_____

_____

_____

God Forgave:

Another point to remember related to forgiveness is the great price that Jesus paid to forgive you of your sins. Think about the mistakes that you have made, but God was able to forgive you.

- Have you truly accepted God's forgiveness for your life?

_____

_____

_____

_____

Consequences of Holding a Grudge:

I.   Lost time stewing over event
II. Living the offense over and over each day
III. Loss of emotional control
IV. Seeds of hatred will grow
V.   Negative impact on health
VI. Broken fellowship with God

How do I know I Have Forgiven?

Now, let's look at some signs that could be good indicators of moving through the forgiveness process.

No longer think about the event day and night	No longer have to talk about the event all the time	No longer feel the need to seek revenge
Can recall those who hurt you, and pray for their well being	No longer get annoyed when their name is mentioned	No longer rejoice when bad things happen

More Discussions:

History:

1. How was forgiveness handled in the home where you grew up?

_____

_____

_____

_____

2. As a child, what lessons did you learn about forgiveness?

_____

_____

_____

_____

3. Did your mother and father practice forgiveness toward each other?

_____

_____

_____

_____

Important Questions:

1. Are there acts your partner could commit that you would not be able to forgive?

_____

_____

_____

_____

2. How will you discuss (with your partner) acts that offend you?

_____

_____

_____

_____

3. How do you respond when you offend your mate?

_____

_____

_____

_____

4. Please describe an issue in your relationship that required you to ask for forgiveness. How did you handle the situation?

_____

_____

_____

_____

5. When you commit an offense or hurt your partner, do you normally initiate the process to ask for forgiveness?

_____

_____

_____

_____

6. Are there issues in the relationship currently, which you feel requires your partner to ask for forgiveness? Describe the situation(s) below:

_____

_____

_____

_____

7. Are there issues in the relationship currently, which requires you to ask for forgiveness? Describe the situation(s) below:

_____

_____

_____

_____

8. How has God forgiven you?

_____

_____

_____

_____

Biblical Wisdom:

Take time to discuss the principles below: What is your interpretation of each? How will you incorporate them into your marriage?

Forgive us our debts, as we also have forgiven our debtors. {Matthew 6:12}

For if you forgive men when they sin against you, your heavenly Father will also forgive you. But if you do not forgive men their sins, your Father will not forgive your sins. {Matthew 6:14-15}

And when you stand praying, if you hold anything against anyone, forgive him, so that your Father in heaven may forgive your sins. {Mark 11:25}

Then Peter came to Jesus and asked, "Lord, how many times shall I forgive my brother when he sins against me? Up to seven times?" Jesus answered, "I tell you not seven times, but seventy-seven times. {Matthew 18:21-22)}

Jesus said, "Father, forgive them, for they do not know what they are doing." {Luke 23:34}

Be kind and compassionate to one another, forgiving each other, just as in Christ God forgave you. {Ephesians 4:32}

COMMITMENT

LASTING A LIFETIME

Rick and Wanda
Married 43 years

LASTING A LIFETIME:

Commitment:

Commitment is inherent in the most fundamental definition of marriage found in the bible. "For this reason a man will leave his father and mother and be united to his wife, and they will become one flesh." (Genesis 2:24) This decision is presented as a once and for all experience.

A marriage commitment is a promise; it is built on a covenant between marital partners, and God. From Genesis to Revelation, the bible intertwines God's marriage covenant to His people with our marriage covenant to our spouses.

- How do you define commitment?

_____

_____

_____

_____

- What does a marriage commitment mean to you?

_____

_____

_____

_____

- How does this marriage commitment rank in priority to all your other commitments?

_____

_____

_____

_____

Permanence of Marriage

The marriage commitment provides us with a clue to understanding the heart of God. It helps us understand what God has done, is doing, and will do for us. It tells us that God's covenant love is a love "that will not let us go." By helping us understand the purpose and permanence of God's relationship with us, the metaphor of the marriage covenant helps us also to understand the purpose and permanence of our marital relationship.

Questions for You:

Review the statements below: Put a (SA) if you strongly agree. Put a (A) if you agree. Put a (D) if you disagree. Put a (SD) if you strongly disagree

1. _____ I feel an extreme level of satisfaction in the relationship right now
2. _____ I have moved from acting, based on self-interest, to acting based on maximizing joint outcomes
3. _____ My partner has moved from acting, based on self-interest, to acting based on maximizing joint outcomes
4. _____ I have a good track record of finishing what I've started
5. _____ I feel comfortable creating long term goals for this marriage
6. _____ I know I am prepared to seek my partner's welfare
7. _____ I am personally prepared to sacrifice for our relationship
8. _____ I am personally dedicated to improving our relationship for the mutual benefit of both of us
9. _____ I am personally prepared to invest in our relationship

THE LOVE TESTER:

Commitment is the great love tester. To love somebody, is to give yourself to meeting their needs for a lifetime. The real test of commitment will be in your dedication, sacrifice, and love during stressful times such as sickness, misunderstanding, and periods of lack. Commitment to a loved one is not dependent on personality. It is a voluntary choice.

• How do you know your partner will be there for you in the future?

_____
_____
_____
_____

• How do you know you have made this relationship a priority in your life?

_____
_____
_____
_____

Keeping Your Word:

Keeping commitments means keeping your word. It is the quality of wholeheartedly and sincerely carrying out duties and responsibilities in the midst of adversity or temptation. It is measured and affirmed through time by the loyalty and trust that is built.

Commitment Building Blocks:

Below you will find some of the characteristics of a true commitment.

Dedication: (being loyal to partner and marriage	Devotion-(attachment to partner and marriage)	Love for- (partner, marriage)
Sacrifice- (putting marriage and partner needs above your own)	Mutually Dependen- (depending on each other)	Investment in (partner, marriage)

More Discussions:

History:
A. How did your mother and father handle commitments?

_____

_____

_____

_____

B. Were commitments discussed in your household growing up?

_____

_____

_____

_____

C. What were some of your commitments growing up?

_____

_____

_____

_____

D. What commitments have you broken in the past?

_____

_____

_____

_____

E. What bad examples did you observe related to commitment growing up?

_____

_____

_____

_____

Important Questions:

1. List five of your current commitments?

_____

_____

_____

_____

2. Have you had someone break a commitment to you? How did this impact you?

_____

_____

_____

_____

3. How does your future spouse view commitment?

_____

_____

_____

_____

4. What fears do you have related to making a lifelong marriage commitment?

_____

_____

_____

_____

5. Why are you totally committed to the success of your marriage?

_____

_____

_____

_____

6. What steps will you put in place to guard your marriage from sexual unfaithfulness?

_____

_____

_____

_____

7. List three ways you know this relationship is developing and progressing.

_____

_____

_____

_____

8. What behavior has your partner displayed that builds your security in this relationship?

_____

_____

_____

_____

9. How do you know, you and your partner display the same level of commitment to this relationship?

_____

_____

_____

_____

10. How would you describe your commitment to God?

_____

_____

_____

_____

Biblical Wisdom:

Take time to discuss the principles below:
What is your interpretation of each?
How will you incorporate them into your marriage?

Commitment: Stays the Course:

The prophet Habakkuk models an essential truth about commitment, "Though the fig tree does not bud and there are no grapes on the vines, though the olive crop fails and the fields produce no food, though there are no sheep in the pen and no cattle in the stalls, yet I will rejoice in the Lord, I will be joyful in God my savior." (Habakkuk 3:17-18)

The key ingredient to Habakkuk's statement is it's unidirectional; he promised to maintain his attitude regardless of the payback. This is a picture of what marriage commitment means.

Christ has made a commitment to us:

"God demonstrates His own love for us: While we were still sinners, Christ died for us." Romans 5:8

Commitment Requires a Single Focus:

"He is a double-minded man, unstable in all he does." James 1:8

Wavering commitment is usually seen as no commitment at all. You only achieve a reputation for commitment through determination and persistence. Genuine commitment stands the test of time. Commitment Requires Improvement: An action underlying commitment is called improving. Improving causes our commitment to be stretched to a higher level. When we are committed to something there is a willingness to look for a better way of doing things. This focus on improvement eliminates complacency, and gives a process to confront what is not working. It builds optimism for the future, while removing dissatisfaction in the past.

COUPLE TESTIMONY

Commitment

Married for 33 Years:

Our definition of commitment is a promise made to each other to be dedicated, devoted, and loyal. Commitment also is honoring God with what he has called you to do or be and staying faithful to the call which brings glory and honor to God.

Being committed to my wife has changed my lifestyle. It has made me more responsible and has helped build character in my life.

Being committed to my husband has taught me how to love through good and bad times. My husband's love and commitment in our marriage has helped me to trust him and has proven that he truly loves me and will be there for me no matter what. His love and commitment for me has changed my love for him tremendously! I wanted to love and be faithful to my husband even more. I can truly say that it made me to be a better person, wife, and mother.

The advice that we would give engaged couples is; **commitment begins when you become engaged.** If you know that you are not going to be committed during the engagement then put the engagement off and work on being committed to that person. Remember commitment is a big part of marriage.

Our advice to married couples would be; you vowed to honor, love and be committed to your spouse. Therefore, you must commit to your call of duty. If you have truly been called to be a husband or wife, then it is your duty to be devoted, dedicated, and loyal to your spouse. "Therefore what God has joined together, let not man separate." Mark 10:9

Rick & Wanda

IN LAWS
ESTABLISHING GROUND RULES

Harry & Chandra
Married 15 Years

IN-LAWS:

The Bible makes note of several supportive in-law relationships, namely: Ruth and Naomi, Moses and his father-in-law Jethro who provided guidance and wisdom to Moses, also Peter and his mother-in-law. The bible also makes notes of other in-law relationships that were not supportive, such as David's father-in-law King Saul, who tracked him down to kill him.

In-law conflicts are not new. They occur in many forms and for various reasons. These conflicts can add heavy stress and pressure to your marriage. They can also create a division between the two of you.

- Have you met your future in-laws?

_____

_____

_____

_____

- How is your relationship with your future in-laws?

_____

_____

_____

_____

- Do your future in-laws support your upcoming marriage?

_____

_____

_____

_____

Part of the Package:

When you marry your partner, their family becomes part of the package. Good in-laws that understand their roles and provide room for the marriage to grow can make married life better. A dysfunctional family or parents that openly show hostility toward a mate can weaken a marriage. All of these issues must be handled constructively. Navigating in-law relationships can be a tricky area in marriage, it requires forethought, honesty, courage, and love. It also has the potential to yield great rewards.

I.   Do the both of you have a game plan in place to deal with in-law conflict?

_____

_____

_____

_____

Boundaries:

You need to do your utmost to be gracious, open, and generous to your in-laws. This is the sort of giving and receiving that makes a family operate effectively. However, the both of you need to have a conversation about what you will and won't do when it comes to in-laws, and establish clear boundaries.

Ground Rules:

One of the best ways to handle in-law conflicts and issues is to establish boundaries and ground rules prior to the marriage.
For the next several questions, please choose a number from 1-10 and write it next to each statement to indicate how much you agree with that statement:

1	2	3	4	5	6	7	8	9	10
Disagree		Somewhat Disagree		Somewhat agree		Agree		Strongly Agree	

1. ____ The both of you should put the needs of your spouse (and the children) above those of other family members.

2. ___ The two of you alone must determine guidelines and agreements for the household you share.

3. ____ The both of you should decide how to raise your children and how much access in-laws will have to the children.

COUPLE TESTIMONY

In-Laws

Married for 20 years:

In-Laws can be a blessing or they can be challenging. When you think about it, without the in-laws we would not have met the spouse of our dreams. They are the ones that provided the resources and tools that have influenced each of us today. They can also give wisdom and insight as they have traveled the road that we are on now. **It is so important though to set guidelines as to how our relationship would be with our in-laws.**

We chose early on that our in-laws would be a blessing to our marriage and made a commitment on the involvement of our in-laws in our marriage. Our first commitment was that we would never discuss our problems with our in-laws as we did not want them to have a biased perspective of the issue or our spouse. **The next commitment is that we would not ever speak negatively or degrade each other in front of the in-laws as this opens the door for misinterpretation of our relationship by them.** Lastly, we would never borrow any money or speak to them about our finances. This keeps this sensitive issue within the confines of our own home. For over 20 years, we have had a great relationship with our in-laws on both sides because of our commitments we made early.

Carlos & Katherine

COMMUNICATION

Carlos and Katherine
Married 31 Years

COMMUNICATION:

Communication in a relationship is a function of emotional connection. When people feel connected, they communicate fine, and when they feel disconnected, they communicate poorly, regardless of their choice of words and communication techniques.

- What does communication mean to you?

_____

_____

_____

_____

- What topics do you and your partner discusses most? (Do not include plans for up-coming wedding)

_____

_____

_____

_____

- Does one of you have a tendency to talk more than the other?

_____

_____

_____

_____

- Do you and your partner talk to each other about the events of your day?

_____

_____

_____

_____

Holding it Together:

Communication is the mortar that holds a relationship together. If it breaks down, the relationship will crumble. When spouses no longer communicate, marriage nurtures no one. It is no longer a marriage.

- Explain how you keep the lines of communication open in your relationship?

_____
_____
_____
_____

- How important is it for you to know your partners perspective?

_____
_____
_____
_____

- What do you appreciate most about your partner's communication?

_____
_____
_____
_____

- How do you react when people do not understand the message you are conveying?

_____
_____
_____
_____

Elements of Communication:

Adapted from Albert Mehrabian, Professor Emeritus of Psychology, UCLA *Please note the % quoted is only accurate when conversations deal with feelings and attitudes

There are basically three elements in any face to face communication:

Words
Tone of Voice
Body Language

These three elements account differently for the meaning of the message:

Words account for 7%
Tone of voice accounts for 38%
Body language accounts for 55%

Goal of Communication:

Effective communication consist of "speaking, listening and responding" it sounds simple and straight forward, but actually communication is a skill which takes practice to be effective. The goal should always be to understand your mate, and make yourself understood by your mate.

• Discuss the communication between you and your partner during social settings?

_____

_____

_____

_____

• How important is it for you to give feedback during conversations with your partner?

_____

_____

_____

_____

4 stages of the listening process:

Without listening there is no real communication

Stage 1– Receiving	Involves the basic need to hearing the right conversation as to what the other person wants to say or express.
Stage 2– Processing	This activity takes place in your mind and involves analyzing, evaluating, and synthesizing
Stage 3– Remembering	This involves remembering information the speaker has conveyed.
Stage 4– Responding	This stage requires that the receiver complete the process through feedback. This is the only way the speaker knows the degree of success in transmitting the message.

- What role does listening play in your relationship with your partner?

_____

_____

_____

_____

- Why is the listening process so hard?

_____

_____

_____

_____

- How does listening play into your relationship with God?

_____

_____

_____

_____

- Does listening require your full attention?

_____

_____

_____

_____

10 Barriers to Effective Communication:

Recognizing barriers to effective communication is a first step in improving your communication style.

◊	Making Assumptions	◊	Blaming/ being defensive
◊	Jumping to conclusions	◊	Demanding/ Ordering
◊	Finishing the Other's Sentences	◊	Harsh Language
◊	Interrupting	◊	Criticizing
◊	Tuning Out	◊	Preparing Response, while they are still speaking.

- How many of the barriers do you recognize from your communication style?

_____

_____

_____

_____

- How many do you recognize from your partner's communication style?

_____

_____

_____

_____

Communication Patterns:

No marriage is without conflict. Many decisions that have to be made in a marriage can often lead to heated debates. A good indicator of the strength of a marriage is the communication pattern used during times of differences. The key is to learn to identify negative communication patterns and replace it with patterns that allow you to respond with love and respect to your mate.

The following exercise will help you identify communication patterns and difficulties. Please read over the below statements, if the action listed is a behavior that you display during heated conversations, please check the "true" box. If it's not a behavior you display, please check the "false" box. Also in the box for" partner" rate your future spouse on each one of these statements.

1. I often find myself name calling, rolling eyes, or interrupting

You	O TRUE	O FALSE
Partner	O TRUE	O FALSE

2. Often I find myself raising my voice

You	O TRUE	O FALSE
Partner	O TRUE	O FALSE

3. I speak before thinking through the issue

You	O TRUE	O FALSE
Partner	O TRUE	O FALSE

4. My Speech is often defensive

You	O TRUE	O FALSE
Partner	O TRUE	O FALSE

5. Once I get started in an argument, I have trouble stopping

You	O TRUE	O FALSE
Partner	O TRUE	O FALSE

6. I try to repay insult with insult

You	O TRUE	O FALSE
Partner	O TRUE	O FALSE

7. I state my complaints in a heated manner

You	O TRUE	O FALSE
Partner	O TRUE	O FALSE

8. I tend to say "you always or "you never" during our heated conversations

You	O TRUE	O FALSE
Partner	O TRUE	O FALSE

9. I often find myself criticizing my partners point of view

You	O TRUE	O FALSE
Partner	O TRUE	O FALSE

10. I get angry quickly during our heated conversations

You	O TRUE	O FALSE
Partner	O TRUE	O FALSE

Communicating From the Heart:

A lot of research has been done about the various levels of communication in a marriage relationship. The best place for a couple to be is an environment where each partner can talk freely, openly and feel safe sharing their most private thoughts. They have learned to stay away from attacking each other, and saying harsh and hurtful comments. When couples communicate at this level, it becomes easier to connect on an intimate level.

Many couples come to the marriage relationship either afraid, or simply not knowing how to be vulnerable with their mate and share openly. Working through the below questions should help you identify areas that might prevent you from sharing openly, and also might prevent you from creating an environment for your mate to share openly.

Please look over the below statements, if this applies to you during normal or heated conversations with your partner, check "true." Check "false" for those that do not apply to you.

i. I often will not express how I really feel

    O TRUE   O FALSE

ii. I protect my true feelings to prevent rejection

    O TRUE   O FALSE

iii. I find it difficult to talk about sensitive topics

    O TRUE   O FALSE

iv. I have a tendency to lie about certain situations to avoid conflict

    O TRUE   O FALSE

v. I often get angry when my mate has a different opinion than mine

    O TRUE   O FALSE

vi. I can comfortably verbalize my concerns

    O TRUE   O FALSE

vii. I can comfortably discuss my needs with my mate

    O TRUE   O FALSE

Speak the Truth in Love:

The truth sometimes can be very unpleasant. This is probably why God says it must be spoken in love. When you speak the truth in love you display a genuine concern for the other person. You are not doing it to get revenge, be hurtful, or to relieve your conscience of guilt, but the goal is to move to complete openness and total intimacy.

To build a satisfying marriage you have to be able to share truthfully and in a loving manner; about your fears, desires, needs, sex, money, weaknesses, mistakes, resentments, etc.: A lot of issues in marriage could be resolved by couple's being honest with each other.

Choose your Words Carefully:

Do you remember as a child hearing the phase "sticks and stones can break my bones, but words will never hurt me?" As an adult we know that harsh and unkind words can hurt very deeply. The book of Proverbs reminds us that "the tongue has the power of life and death." The book of James tells us that the human tongue, though a small part of the body, it has the power to make a tremendous impact. Words carry a lot of power.

Once words are spoken, they cannot be erased. The effects of harsh words can linger for a long period of time. The best way to avoid this type of pain is to choose our words carefully. Couples that communicate to each other in harsh language or unkind words will create a battle field in their marriage.

More Discussions:

History:
1. Describe communication between your mother and father.

_____

_____

_____

_____

2. What communication habits did you learn in the home where you grew up?

_____

_____

_____

_____

3. How was your communication with your family and relatives growing up?

_____

_____

_____

_____

4. Were needs and feelings openly expressed in the home where you grew up?

_____

_____

_____

_____

5. When did you start praying to God?

_____

_____

_____

_____

Important Questions:

a. List the areas of communication in your relationship that needs improvement.

_____

_____

_____

_____

b. What would you change about your partner's communication style?

_____

_____

_____

_____

c. What improvements do you need to make related to your listening skills?

_____

_____

_____

_____

d. How will you maintain open and honest communication with your partner?

_____

_____

_____

_____

e. Can you think of a past situation that caused you to communicate to your mate in a harsh and unloving manner?

_____

_____

_____

_____

f. Can you think of a past situation that caused your mate to communicate to you in a harsh and unloving manner?

_____

_____

_____

_____

g. Do you and your partner spend a lot of time talking about past mistakes and failures?

_____

_____

_____

_____

h. Do you feel your confidential disclosures are safe with your partner?

_____

_____

_____

_____

i. Do you use the silent treatment as a means to avoid difficult topics?

_____

_____

_____

_____

Biblical Wisdom:

Take time to discuss the principles below:

What is your interpretation of each?

How will you incorporate them into your marriage?

A word aptly spoken is like apples of gold in a setting of silver. (Proverbs 25: 11)

My dear brothers, take note of this: everyone should be quick to listen, slow to speak and slow to become angry. (James 1:19)

All kinds of animals, birds, reptiles and creatures of the sea are being tamed and have been tamed by man. But no man can tame the tongue. It is a restless evil, full of deadly poison. (James 3: 7-8)

A gentle answer turns away wrath, but a harsh word stirs up anger. (Proverbs 15:1)

Do not let any unwholesome talk come out of your mouths, but only what is helpful for building others up according to their needs, that it may benefit those who listen. (Ephesians 4:29)

Pleasant words are a honey comb, sweet to the soul and healing to the bones. (Proverbs 16:24)

Notes

SOCIAL MEDIA

Khaleb and Jori
Married 1 Year

SOCIAL MEDIA

1. Are you a social media user?

_____

_____

_____

_____

_____

2. Which platform do you use (Facebook, Instagram, YouTube, TikTok, WhatsApp, etc..)

_____

_____

_____

_____

_____

3. On average, how many hours do you entertain social media (outside of work)?

_____

_____

_____

_____

_____

4. In what ways can social media benefit you in your relationship and marriage?

_____

_____

_____

_____

5. In what ways can social media hurt you in your relationship and marriage?

_____

_____

_____

_____

6. What are your thoughts on your partner having access to all your social media accounts?

_____

_____

_____

_____

_____

7. Why is it important to have access to your partner's social media accounts?

_____

_____

_____

_____

_____

8. How will you protect your relationship and marriage from social media?

_____

_____

_____

_____

_____

9. What boundaries would you like to set with your partner concerning social media?

_____

_____

_____

_____

_____

10. What will be your commitment to your partner as it relates to social media?

_____

_____

_____

_____

_____

5 STAGES OF TRUST

Robert and Robin
Married 16 Years

TRUST DEFINED

Trust is a choice to be available, vulnerable and transparent in a relationship, because the person you're trusting has proven worthy of your partnership through consistency in their honest, integrity and dependability."

Based on this simple definition of trust, we see that trust is much more than a gut feeling or a blind faith in someone. It's merit-based. For this reason, trust is completely different than love and forgiveness. Love and forgiveness can't be earned (only given freely), but trust can't be given freely; it must be earned. Trust is the only vital part of a relationship that must be earned. We don't have to trust someone in order to love or forgive them, but love and forgiveness are vital to allowing trust to have the opportunit to be rebuilt when its been broken.

STAGE 1: CONNECTION

We're drawn to someone and feel a "connection" which propels us to start the process of building a relationship (whether a romantic relationship, a friendship, a business relationship/ partnership, etc). The connection motivates us to invest the time necessary.

STAGE 2: CAUTION

We cautiously start to pursue the possibility of trust in this fledgling relationship. We start creating opportunities where we can observe this person' character in action and allow them to view the same in us. We're careful to proceed with caution and patience, because the process of building trust is delicate and it requires time.

STAGE 3: CONSISTENCY

This is where trust turly begins to form. Consistency is the primary ingredient of trust. When we observe consistency in honest words and actions from someone, we naturally let our guard down and can experience the deeper levels of relational intimacy trust always makes possible. Their consistence gives us the courage to take the next step.

STAGE 4: COURAGE

Trust is rooted in viewing consistency in another person, but it still requires an element of faith and courage. This is the point in the relationship where we're ready to put our heart on the line (or money on the line if it's a business relationship/partnership).

We're willing to assume some risk (which is required in every relationship) because we now feel safe and secure with this person.

STAGE 5: COMMITMENT

Our courage to trust always leads to a commitment. Every relationship requires some level of commitment, and the level of our commitment will ultimately define the level of our commitment will ultimately define the level of our relationship. This is more pronounced in a marriage relationship where the commitment is a sacred, lifelong vow, but even in friendship and business relationships, some level of commitment is always required.

Whenever trust is broken in a relationship, we must always return to the second stage and proceed with caution to allow trust to be rebuilt through the remaining stages.

MATCH THE STATEMENTS BELOW:

I'm ready to be with this person because we enjoy each other and feel safe.

Commitment

I promise to be faithful and loyal to you for the rest of my life

Consistency

Your love never changes. You constantly show that you're there for me

Connection

We have so much in common and looking forward to our next date

Caution

Not sure if I'm ready to be in a committed relationship, taking it slow

Courage

MARRIAGE VISION & MISSION STATEMENTS

Rocky and Lani
Married 32 Years

MARRIAGE STATEMENTS & GOALS

Now let's take time to create a vision statement, a mission statement, and also list some goals for your marriage. You and your partner should work on these tasks together.

Marriage Vision Statement

Proverbs 29:18a - Where there is no vision, the people perish.

A vision statement is a picture of your marriage in the future. Your marriage vision statement should serve as your inspiration, and consist of your dreams and hopes for your marriage. It should also answer the question "where do you want your marriage to go."

A clear vision statement for your marriage can keep you moving forward, unify your expectations, and provide a roadmap to assess if you are on course in your relationship. Couples who have a joint vision for life can accomplish so much more as a team.

➡️ Write your statement in positive terms, it should state what you want, not what you don't want. Make it specific, short, direct, focused and use "we Statements".

Our Vision Statement

_____

_____

_____

_____

Marriage Mission Statement

Ephesians 5:1- Be imitators of God, therefore, as dearly loved children.

While a vision statement tells where you want the marriage to go, a mission statement outlines how our marriage will represent Christ and serve as a picture of ministry.

A mission statement helps you to focus on how you want your marriage to bear fruit for

Christ. It answers the question what has God called our marriage to represent to others for His kingdom.

Our Mission Statement:

_____

_____

_____

_____

_____

Goals

One of the concepts that keep a marriage moving in a forward direction, and improve its level of success is that of goal setting. Goals can be the catalyst to help energize and motivate you to achieve.

By having clear goals, couples know what they are striving to achieve. Goals give you a stronger focus, and increase your efficiency by organizing your time and resources. A great way to lay out goals is to make them SMART. See acronym below:

S - SPECIFIC - What do I want to accomplish, by when and how will I do it.

M - MEASURABLE - Establish concrete criteria for measuring progress toward the attainment of your goals.

A- ACHIEVABLE - Are you willing and able to make the commitment to achieving your goal.

R - RELEVANT- Your goals should be relevant to your life, other priorities, and your dedication to God.

T - TIME BOUND - Your goals should be grounded within time frames (what date will they be achieved). Without a time frame there is no sense of urgency.

Now let's start the process of you and your partner setting goals for your marriage. The goals you list should consist of both joint and personal goals. By listing your personal goals, you are keeping your mate in the loop. You can also determine if personal goals conflict with joint goals, or if they need to be adjusted. You will separate your goals into four time frames; goals you would like to achieve in the next 3, 5, 7 and 10 years.

➡️ Write your goals down, and review them frequently!

Our Goals to Achieve in the Next 3 Years:

_____

_____

_____

_____

Our Goals to Achieve in the Next 5 Years:

_____

_____

_____

_____

Our Goals to Achieve in the Next 7 Years:

_____

_____

_____

_____

Our Goals to Achieve in the Next 10 Years:

_____

_____

_____

_____

_____

_____

_____

_____

_____

_____

_____

_____

YOUR HEALTH

Joey and Jill
Married 10 Years

<u>Health</u>

0   1   2   3   4   5   6   7   8   9   10

1. On a scale from 1 to 10 (1 being terrible, 10 being great) how would you rate your partner's overall health? If below 5, please rate your concern.

_____

_____

_____

_____

2. What are your thoughts on healthy eating?

_____

_____

_____

_____

3. What are your thoughts on exercise?

_____

_____

_____

_____

4. Do you prefer alternative or modern medicine?

_____

_____

_____

_____

5. Do you know your partner's health history?

_____

_____

_____

_____

• We strongly encourage you to exchange health records with your partner and make changes if necessary to build a strong and healthy marriage.

DECISION MAKING

Brian and Coretta
Married 27 Years

DECISION MAKING:

No matter where you are in life or what position you hold; you make decisions every day. Some decisions you make have a greater impact than others, but the skill to reach a conclusion is the same. A business can fail or succeed based on the quality of the decision making process.

A marriage relationship is no different. The decision making process is an important element to its success. Each day, the two of you will be presented with problems and challenges that require you to use your decision making skills. The goal is to make good decisions; consistently making poor decisions is bad for the relationship.

• What is your decision making style?

_____
_____
_____
_____

• How do you react when you have to make decisions under short time restraints?

_____
_____
_____
_____

What's Important?

Some decisions are made automatically and do not require input from each other, such as brushing your teeth at night. Some decisions have a short impact on your life, while others have a more lasting impact. What you consider to be important decisions and the process you will use to make decision making clear is one of the first decisions you should make.

As you join your lives together, it's important to identify those decisions that you consider major or important. Identifying those in the beginning will help reduce stress as these topics come up in the future. By identifying these topics you are saying we must decide as a team the right course of action.

Below is a list of some of the decisions that most couples say require discussion and agreement:

1. Where the two of you will live
2. How many children will we have
3. What parenting style will we use
4. How will we spend and save money
5. How will we split the household chores
6. Making future plans
7. Decisions regarding a crisis
8. Who will work
9. Right time to purchase home
10. Starting a new career
11. What Church to attend

Please use the space below to make a list of decisions that you consider major and or important and require discussion and agreement.

1. _____
_____

2. _____
_____

3. _____
_____

4. _____
_____

5. _____
_____

6. _____
_____

7. _____
_____

8. _____
_____

9. _____

   _____

10. _____

   _____

What They Reveal:

Decisions can reveal our values, priorities, and character. Good decision making require an obedience to and dependence upon God. Good decisions demand wisdom.

- What is God's role in your decision making process?

  _____

  _____

  _____

  _____

- What process do you and your partner use to make decisions?

  _____

  _____

  _____

  _____

God Honoring Decisions:

No decision is wise if it's made independent of God. Below you'll find a biblical model for making God honoring decisions:

1. **Pray for Wisdom**- Difficult decisions begin with prayer. Ask for God's wisdom right from the start. Solomon referred to this as committing your works to God.

   "Commit your works to the Lord, and your plans will be established"- Proverbs 16:3

2. **Gather Information**- Information allows you to have a careful, thought-through, informed decision. With the absence of information you can't weigh all available options. This phase should also include identifying the people this decision impacts.
   "Every prudent man acts with knowledge"- Proverbs 13:16

3. **Seek Godly Counsel-** Godly counsel can give us a different perspective, and also a place to examine our motives. The key term is "Godly counsel." It is imperative when seeking counsel that you know the character and values of the person you receive advice. You also must evaluate the advice you receive to make sure it fits the word of God.

   "Plans fail for lack of counsel, but with many advisers they succeed"- Proverbs 15:22

4. **Search the Bible-** Before making a difficult decision we must search God's word to see if the bible tells us what to do. Often the bible will speak directly to our situation, and if it does not speak directly to our situation, more than likely there are principles that speak indirectly to our issue. No matter how obvious a decision seems, it is never right to make a decision contrary to what God has commanded.

   "There is no wisdom, no insight, no plan that can succeed against the Lord"- Proverbs 21:30

5. **Choose a course of action-** When all things have been evaluated, there is the point where you must make the decision. This course of action should stand when evaluated by what the bible says.

   "All hard work brings a profit, but mere talk leads to poverty"- Proverbs 14:23

Mutual Decision Making:

Sharing and participating together as partners in decision making can build interdependence and connection with one another. On the other hand, not sharing this process can weaken a marriage and create a one-sided advantage in the marriage. Mutual decision making creates an environment for both partners to participate.

Find some elements of the mutual decision making process below

- Making decisions should be a shared responsibility

- Both partners should be sincerely concerned about the wishes and personal preferences of the other.

- The decision making process should not be a competition.

- Listen to each other's point of view. Seeking more to understand than to be understood. • Come to the discussion with complete honesty about your point of view.

- Allow your partner to come to the discussion with complete honesty about their point of view.

More Discussions:

History:

1. Who made most of the decisions in your home?

_____

_____

_____

2. How did your parents react when you made a bad decision?

_____

_____

_____

3. What did you learn about decision making as a teenager?

_____

_____

_____

4. How was decision making handled in your past relationships?

_____

_____

_____

Important Questions:

1. List (3) to (5) bad decisions you have made in the past.

   _____

   _____

   _____

2. How do you react when you make a bad decision?

   _____

   _____

   _____

3. Do you typically allow others to make major decisions for you?

   _____

   _____

   _____

4. Have you had to make decisions that impacted others? Explain;

   _____

   _____

   _____

5. Give your thoughts on your partner's decision making abilities?

   _____

   _____

   _____

6. What role will prayer play in your decision making process?

   _____

   _____

   _____

7. List any major decisions that you and your partner will have to make immediately after you are married?

   _____

   _____

   _____

8. How will you and your partner honor God through your decisions?

_____

_____

_____

9. Who in your circle do you trust to give you wise counsel?

_____

_____

_____

10. What process will you follow when both of you disagree, and a decision has to be made?

_____

_____

_____

Biblical Wisdom:

Take time to discuss the principles below:
What is your interpretation of each?
How will you incorporate them into your marriage?

"Can two walk together, except they are agreed?"- Amos 3:3 (KJV)

Decision making is an agreement process, if you come away from the table with two different resolutions to the issue you will go in different directions.

"Then make my joy complete by being like-minded, having the same love, being one in spirit and purpose"- Philippians 2:2

"Do nothing out of selfish ambition or vain conceit, but in humility consider others better than yourselves. Each of you should look not only to your own interests, but also to the interests of others"- Philippians 2:3-4 71

"Two are better than one; because they have a good return for their work"- Ecclesiastes 4:9

COUPLE TESTIMONY

Decision Making

Married 5.5 Years:

Decision making in a marriage is very important. It's important because it teaches communication, compromise and allows opportunities to express different opinions, perceptions, etc. **Through effective decision making, couples can learn more about each other's values, hot buttons, dreams, and expectations.**

Our approach to decision making is to use a list of pros and cons, allow each person to voice their perspective, do research, and talk it out and discuses consequences of the decision. However, there is still a challenge when one person feels more strongly about the decision than the other. Or when both feel very strongly but are on opposing ends. **Sometimes it is difficult once a decision is made to feel confident about the joint decision and not second guess the decision.**

When making joint decisions it's important to communicate, listen to where the other person is coming from, compromise (do not argue from your position, but be open to seeing a different perspective). **When you disagree, do so in love and respect for your partner.** Once a decision has been made, be united in your decision. Do not talk negatively to friends or loved ones about the decision you've made as a couple. This may undermine or undervalue your partner and your relationship.

Harry & Chandra

Notes

_____

_____

_____

_____

_____

_____

_____

_____

_____

_____

_____

_____

_____

_____

_____

_____

_____

_____

_____

_____

_____

_____

_____

_____

_____

_____

_____

_____

_____

_____

CONFLICT MANAGEMENT

Larry & Rebecca
Married 32 years

CONFLICT MANAGEMENT:

At some point in your marriage you will have a disagreement or misunderstanding with your spouse. Conflict in marriage is inevitable. Even the best marriages experience conflict from time to time. The key to success is how couples manage their conflict.

- Explain how you typically handle conflict.

_____

_____

_____

- How does your partner typically handle conflict

_____

_____

_____

Dealing with Conflict:

Marital conflicts are not bad in themselves. It is our response to the conflicts that can be either helpful or harmful. Marital conflict can be the challenge to help us grow into more mature persons and a more mature relationship. However, conflict that is not handled effectively can cause negativity to grow in a marriage. Also, on-going unresolved conflict can cause couples to become so indifferent to each other that they stop interacting in a meaningful way.

- Describe a conflict that you handled wrong.

_____

_____

_____

- Describe a conflict that you handled well.

_____

_____

_____

Managed vs. Unmanaged:

Conflict allows both partners to express important feelings and come up with creative solutions to problems. Successfully managed conflict can produce positive outcomes in the relationship.

Managed Conflict	Unmanaged Conflict
Strengthens Relationship and Build Trust	Damages Relationship and discourages Trust
Encourages open communication and cooperative problem solving	Results in opposing defensiveness and hidden agendas
Deals with issues at hand and focus on a win-win solution	Focuses on finger pointing and blaming
Seek to resolve issues in a calm manner	Is often loud, out of control and hostile

Common Areas of Conflict:

Below is a list of common areas of marital conflict:

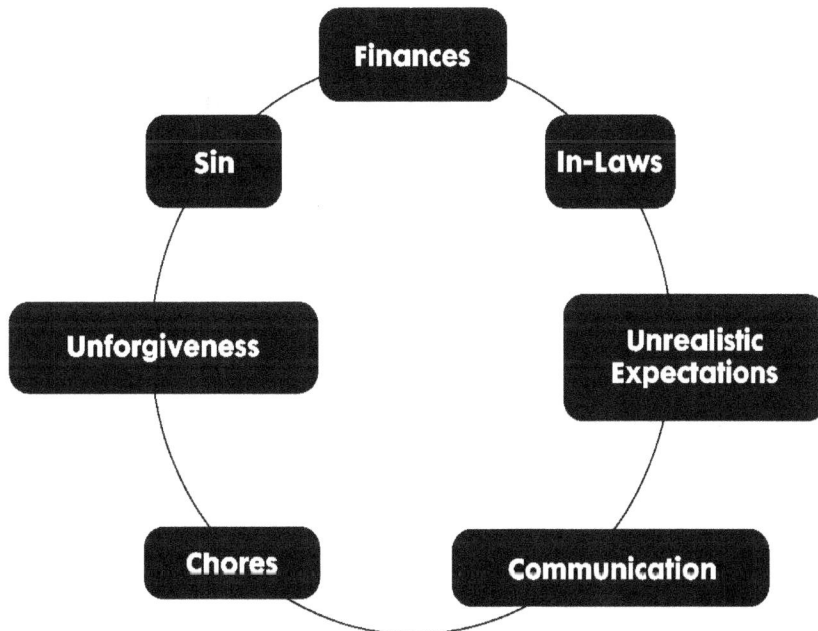

Finances

In-Laws

Unrealistic Expectations

Communication

Chores

Unforgiveness

Sin

Look at the areas above and use this scale to categorize how much you expect each one to be a problem in your marriage.

Also use this scale to categorize how you think your future spouse would rate each area.

	YOU	SPOUSE
A. Finances	_____	_____
B. B. In-Laws	_____	_____
C. Unrealistic Expectations	_____	_____
D. Communication	_____	_____
E. Household Chores	_____	_____
F. Un-forgiveness	_____	_____
G. Un-repented Sin	_____	_____

Sources of Conflict:

Anger & Hate
Proverbs 29:22
An Angry man stirs up dissension, and a hot tempered one commits many sins.

Spiritual Immaturity
1 Corinthians 3:3
You are still worldly. For since there is jealously and quarreling among you, are you not worldly? Are you not acting like mere man?

Unrealized Expectations
Proverbs 13:12
Hope deferred makes the heart sick, but a longing fulfilled is a tree of life. Our expectations need to be tested against God's word.

Selfishness
James 4:1
What causes fights and quarrels among you? Don't they come from your desires that battle within you?

Pride
Proverbs 13:10
Pride only breeds quarrels, but wisdom is found in those who take advice.
The marriage relationship is the place to display humility and not pride.

> A. Look over the above sources of conflict
> B. B. Use the scale below to rate the level each one is present now in your relationship
> C. 1) Not Present 2) Somewhat Present 3) Present 4) Present most of the time 5) Present Always

Rating

1. Anger & Hate   _____

2. Spiritual Immaturity   _____

3. Unrealized Expectations   _____

4. Selfishness   _____

5. Pride   _____

Ways we Deal with Conflict:

Your perception of conflict can be based on past painful memories from previous relationships or childhood. Because of these negative experiences, you can view conflict in your present day relationships as something to fear or avoid. Fearing, avoiding, or addressing conflict in an unhealthy manner will only add additional stress to the marriage.

Now, let's look at some of the common negative ways we deal with conflict. To help you remember these common ways, we have developed an acronym (FLIPS).

F- (FIGHT) - Fight for their way and point of view, refuses to listen to the other side.
L- (LIE) - Afraid to speak the truth in love. Lies about the issue, refuses to open up.
I- (IGNORE) - Does not pay attention to the conflict, and takes no action to resolve it.
P- (PRETEND) - Downplays the severity of the issue, and pretends it has no importance.
S- (SETTLE) - Whatever you decide is fine with me. Even if the outcome is damaging and hurtful. Just want the conflict to be over.

- Which method above do you use most often?

_____

_____

_____

- Which method above does your partner use most often?

_____

_____

_____

Healthy Conflict:

Now, let's look at right approaches to conflict. In a healthy marriage, conflict is addressed when both partners work together to manage the issue as partners and not as adversaries. In other words, they focus on managing their differences and not on attacking one another. This allows the marriage to be preserved and strengthen. As you learn and practice healthy conflict management skills, the relationship will grow to a deeper level.

Collaboration:

Using the collaboration process, couples work together as partners to create a solution that they both own. The collaboration process focuses on attacking the problem, rather than each other. In order for this process to work, there are some basics that each partner must bring to the table. **(1) Husbands must come to the table loving their wives, as Christ loved the church. (2) Wives must come to the table respecting their husbands. (3) You must deal only with the issue at hand. (4) Deal with the issue as quickly as possible, and do not allow your anger to pass into another day.** Please find the collaboration process below:

1. Create a Collaborative Environment - Be trustworthy and respect your mate's ideas and opinion.
2. Be Consistent - In your behavior and the way you respond to your partner.
3. Be Humble - Your ideas may be good, but it's also possible your partners ideas could be better.
4. Be Committed - To working together as partners to manage conflict, and accurately identifying the issue.
5. Be Willing - To merge insights, concerns, and different perspectives from your partner into a consensual decision.

More Discussions:

History:

- How was conflict handled in the home where you grew up?

_____

_____

_____

- Did you experience a lot of conflict with family or friends growing up?

_____

_____

_____

- What was your greatest source of conflict as a teenager?

_____

_____

_____

- How have you responded to conflict in your past relationships?

_____

_____

_____

Important Questions:

1. Explain which one is most important to you; managing the conflict? or being right?

_____

_____

_____

_____

2. Discuss some of the major differences you see between you and your partner.

_____

_____

_____

_____

3. Do you see areas where you would like your partner to change after marriage?

_____
_____
_____
_____

4. How do you feel when you lose an argument?

_____
_____
_____
_____

5. Describe a conflict you have had with your future spouse. How was it resolved?

_____
_____
_____
_____

6. How well do you understand your own feelings and needs?

_____
_____
_____
_____

7. How effectively can you communicate your feelings and needs?

_____
_____
_____
_____

8. Do you normally take ownership for your part of the conflict?

_____
_____
_____
_____

9. Describe the last conflict you had with your partner.

_____
_____
_____
_____

10. What are some of the current issues in which you are having disagreements?

_____
_____
_____
_____

Biblical Wisdom:

Take time to discuss the principles below:
What is your interpretation of each?
How will you incorporate them into your marriage?

"A new command I give you; Love one another, as I have loved you, so you must love one another"- John 13:34

An important principle in resolving conflict in marriage is to love one another as Christ has loved the church.

"Examine yourselves to see whether you are in the faith; Test yourselves, do you not realize that Christ Jesus is in you. Unless, of course, you fail the test?" - 2 Corinthians 13:5

When conflict arises do self-examination. After you have brought your concerns to God and been honest with yourself about your own failures and selfish desires, then you can approach your mate with your concerns.

"Do to others as you would have them do to you" - Luke 6:31

Remember as you are trying to manage conflict, treat your mate as you want to be treated.

"He who loves a quarrel loves sin; he who builds a high gate invites destruction" - Proverbs 17:19

COUPLES TESTIMONY

Conflict Management

Married for 11 Years:

Conflict management is first realizing that there will be conflict. No marriage is without conflict. The other part of conflict management is how you choose to handle the conflict. Every couple should work together to determine how to manage conflict in their marriage. We choose to handle conflict by allowing each other a cooling off period before we discuss our concerns. This works for us because this allows us the time to pull together our thoughts and have a rational discussion.

Trying to discuss an issue while either one of us is extremely emotional would lead to one person being defensive and neither party listening. Using the cool off period can be helpful, but it also presents a couple of challenges. One challenge we have faced is waiting too long to discuss a conflict. When we allow problems to fester, issues tend to compound and tension rises in the home. The other challenge we face is finding the right words. During the cool off period we spend time thinking through how to express concerns. If we are not careful about what we say, the other person could be hurt by our words. The last thing we want to do is hurt the one we love.

When it comes to conflict management the advice we would give those that are already married is refrain from cataloging, and don't bring up previously resolved or unrelated topics while handling a specific conflict. Bringing up unrelated topics will divert the discussion and the present issues will not get addressed. Bringing up things that were resolved in the past may raise tension in the discussion and cause you to lose faith in conflict management.

Eddie & Melissa

DEATH BLOWS

Barry and Cathy
Married 34 Years

CRITICIMS

Criticism refers to attacking or putting down your partner's personality or character rather than his or her behavior itself. When you criticize your partner you are basically implying that there is something wrong with him or her. But does that mean that you shouldn't say anything about your partner's behavior that users your? Of course not. Expressing your feelings, even strong, powerful feelings, is fine. But it's how you do it that matters.

CRITICISM VS. COMPLAINTS.

There's a big difference between a complaint and a criticism. A complaint addresses a specific action or non-action and is different to criticism in that a complaint targets a behavior you want to change.

Here is an example:

You have discovered that the toilet seat is up.
Criticism: "What's WRONG with you? Are you that lazy that you won't even put down a toilet seat after you use it?"

Complaint: "The toilet seat is up again. Maybe try to put it down after you use it."

ANTIDOTES TO CRITICISM:

– Find the request, wish and/or need behind the criticism.

– Address the behavior you do not like, do not attack the person.

– Learn to make specific complaints and requests ("When X happened, I felt Y, I want Z")

– Soften your start up. Begin tactfully, be clear and describe what's happening—don't evaluate or judge.

CONTEMPT

Is any statement or nonverbal behavior that attacks your partner's sense of self with the intention to insult or psychologically abuse him orher. It shows blatant disrespect fore your partner and puts you on a higher ground.

Such behaviros include yey rolling, swearing, name calling, hostile humor and sarcasm. Nothing is more destructive to love than contempt.

To fight contempt, couples have to work very hard to create a culture of appreciation. Both of you may be feeling very unappreciated in the relationship. To change this around, it is important to actively chance your mindset.

ANTIDOTES TO CONTEMPT:

– Be aware of your thoughts, feelings and behaviors and understand what it is thatyou are really upset about. Target that rather than using passive-aggressive ways to tell your partner how you feel.

– Speak respectfully even when angry.
—Let go of any unhelpful stories (f righteous indignation or innocent victimization that you are making up and re-write your inner script.

—Practice holding your partner in warm regard, even when feeling distant or during a flight.

—Catch your partner doing something right, and te him other that you appreciate them for what they are doing.

DEFENSIVENESS

Is an attempt to protect yourself, to defend your innocence or to ward off a perceived attack. Making excuses, cross0-complaining and "yes-butting" are all forms of defensive behavior.

When feeling under attack, it's understandable that people get defensive. That's why it is such a difficult habit to break. However, defensiveness rarely works because it's really another form of blaming.

ANITODOTES TO DEFENSIVENESS

– Use active listening: Maybe what you heard isn't what was said. Check out with your partner whether you heard it accurately before you jump into defending yourself.

– Validate what your partner is saying: let your partner know what makes sense to you about what they are saying.

– Accept some responsibility for what your partner is bringing to you. Don't bat it back, don't deny all charges.

– Learn to get 'undefended'. Scan for whatever is valid in your partner's complaint and take responsibility to address it: "What can I learn from this?... What can I do about it? "

STONEWALLING

Stonewalling happens when rather than confronting the issues with your partner, you take evasive action such as tuning out or turning away. Common responses include stony silence, one word answers or changing the subject. There is a reluctance to express directly what you are thinking or feeling

While some people use stonewalling as a way to calm themselves or the situation down, it seldom works because your partner is likely to assume you don't care enough about the problem to talk about it and finds it very upsetting to be ignored.

ANTIDOTES TO STONEWALLING:

– Check for feelings of being emotionally overwhelmed (i.e. emotional flooding).

– Take time out: Tell your partner you need a break from the conflict discussion. You can disengage from the conversationwith a phrase such as "Let's leave this for another time, when we're calmer."

– Assure your partner that you will return to the conversation when you're both ready.

– During your time out, do something soothing or calming such as listening to music or reading a magazine. Try taking several slow, deep breaths.

– Address your fear/s of what will happen if you express your thoughts and feelings directly to your partner.

PARENTING/ BLENDED FAMILY

Michael and Michelle
Married 15 Years

PARENTING:

Parenting is possibly one of the most important jobs and roles to play. Effective parenting is very important to a family's success; it also shapes how the future generation will behave. It is more than simple biology, but should be a process to teach children who they are, whose they are, where they belong, and why they are here. The most important element is for you and your spouse to be a unified front on your approach to parenting.

Important Conversation:

Before you get married, you and your mate should have a conversation about if you plan to have children, if so; how many, and when do you plan to start the process. Having children is a long-term commitment, which requires long hours, and financial resources. But the long term benefits can be very rewarding. It's important to have open and honest dialogue about this topic prior to marriage.

Do not assume your mate wishes to have children. Take the time to understand your partners view point and value regarding children. Also, this is the time to put any health issues on the table that might impact or prevent the conception process. The fact that there may be an issue that would prevent a child from being conceived could be a deal breaker for your mate. This is a crucial conversation to have prior to a serious commitment.

Blended/Stepfamilies:

Due to the rising divorce rate, and more people having children before marriage, chances are high that a lot of marriages today may have children from a previous relationship or marriage. Current statistics tells us that blended families are growing by a rate of 1,300 each day. Living in a blended family environment can be a bumpy road. The process of blending two families into one is often extremely challenging. As a new couple from a previous relationship, you face special challenges that are unique to blended families. Forming a healthy stepfamily can take time, and rushing this process may lead to disappointment and cause some family members to resist bonding.

Discuss the Details:

As you and your new spouse work together to establish a new blended family, it's important for the step-parent to understand how issues such as discipline, household rules and each child's responsibilities have been handled in the past. Also it's important to discuss the role of the other biological parent. Are they involved, and to what extent. Do they provide financial support? How is the relationship between parents?

Spend a lot of time talking through these issues, both of you are equally responsible for a balanced, healthy, and fully informed decision. Remember that children have to deal with the decisions of the adults responsible for them. Think about how powerless you would feel in their position, and behave with care, compassion, and concern for them.

Rewarding Experience:

While having a blended family can be difficult and challenging at times, it can also be a wonderful and rewarding experience. You are expanding your family and building relationships and new traditions that will last a lifetime.

More Discussions:

• Have you and your partner had detailed conversations related to having children?

_____

_____

_____

_____

• Are you comfortable with your partner's viewpoint related to having children?

_____

_____

_____

_____

• If you plan to have children, have you discussed the time frame you will start?

_____

_____

_____

_____

- What is your parenting philosophy? Is this different from your mate?

_____

_____

_____

_____

- How do you feel about adoption?

_____

_____

_____

_____

- What does your partner think about adoption?

_____

_____

_____

_____

- To what extent medically, are you willing to go to have a family?

_____

_____

_____

_____

- Will one of you be a stay at home parent? If yes, who? And for how long?

_____

_____

_____

_____

- How will having a child change the way you live now?

_____

_____

_____

_____

- What values do you want to instill in your children?

_____

_____

_____

_____

- What values does your partner want to instill in your children?

_____

_____

_____

_____

- What role will God and faith play into the raising of your children?

_____

_____

_____

_____

Blended/Stepfamilies:

If you are a blended/stepfamily, answer the series of questions below:

- What are your expectations for the blending of your family?

_____

_____

_____

_____

- Have you established house rules you both agree on?

_____

_____

_____

_____

- Have the both of you established a regular family meeting to discuss present and future conflicts that may arise?

  _____
  _____
  _____
  _____

- What things will you do as a family to help the bonding process?

  _____
  _____
  _____
  _____

- Has the step-parent met the other biological parent?

  _____
  _____
  _____
  _____

- What issues do you anticipate from the other biological parent?

  _____
  _____
  _____
  _____

- What do you see as the biggest hurdle to blending your family?

  _____
  _____
  _____
  _____

- How does the child(ren) feel about the marriage?

  _____
  _____
  _____
  _____

Questions for the Step-parent:

- Explain how the child(ren) has changed since you met them?

_____

_____

_____

_____

- How has your relationship with the child(ren) evolved?

_____

_____

_____

_____

- What have you done with the child(ren) that you are most proud of?

_____

_____

_____

_____

- What aspect of your relationship with the child(ren) needs work?

_____

_____

_____

_____

- What type of step-parent will you be?

_____

_____

_____

_____

COUPLES TESTIMONY

Parenting

Married 20 Years:

We vividly remember the birth of both our sons as they were miracles! We were so excited during the birth process and while we were in the hospital. Reality hit when we brought each of them home. There was a wave of emotions that engulfed us; excited, scared, overwhelmed, apprehensive, anxious, and the list goes on and on. Even though we prepared ourselves and took the birthing and parenting classes, now we had to perform! And although others were giving us instructions, we had to depend upon God and ourselves to parent our sons as both were very unique gifts from God, as all children are. We started to realize the following areas and they allowed us to parent in the way we believe God intended.

Parenting is a phased approach: There are different phases that our sons will live through and our responsibility is to guide them through each phase and ultimately help them to become responsible productive men. The phases are baby, infant, toddler, child, pre-teen, young adult, responsible mature adult. Each of these phases is important and as we progress through them, each has their own rewards and challenges. To make it more complicated each son progresses through them differently. Recognizing the phase that our children are in and their own style and personality, determines how we would parent them through it.

There is strength in each of our sons: As parents, there are a ton of comparisons that we unknowingly or unconsciously create when it comes to our children. We compare them to one another, to other children, to images we see on TV, etc. We discovered that there is a uniqueness and purpose for each of our sons which give them their purposeful strength. This is what makes parenting purposeful. We have to truly study our children in order to be able to see it. It is truly a God blessing and it doesn't mean that it does not come with challenges, but there is a journey that gets them closer to their fulfilled purposeful life where we have 90 responsibility in parenting them in reaching it.

Create a village: The famous saying that "it takes a village to raise a child" is so true. What we had to do which was critical was create a village. This village consists of trusted family members, friends, neighbors, church members, our son's friends and parents. This was an intentional safe village created for our sons so that they would be able to flourish, grow, gain exposure and be nurtured in a very positive way. This is even helping today in that it has developed a strengthened confidence in who they are and them knowing that not only are they loved by us, but by the village.

These three areas have focused our efforts and proven positive results on parenting our young men!

Carlos & Katherine

FINANCES

Larry and Rebecca
Married 31 Years

MONEY MATTERS

Money is one of the major causes of frustration in marriage. Couples have to realize the great importance that money plays in a marriage, and learn to define guidelines for money management. It has been noted that money is one of the most significant areas of potential conflict in marriage and is consistently among the top four reasons for divorce.

Money can be valued differently by each individual. To one person money can serve as a means of security, while another person can look to money to make them feel happy. One person can be a saver while the other one is a spender. Money is not a "romantic topic", so most couples fail to discuss this topic before marriage.

It is important for couples to understand how money is valued by the other partner. Couples should lay the cards on the table and commit openly and honestly in discussing their financial position. Couples in successful marriage have mastered the skill of financial harmony in their relationship. Successful couples set guidelines and boundaries for their financial decisions. They understand the value that each partner places on money, and understand that both partners will have equal rights and responsibilities with control of the finances.

Budgets/Financial Plans

One of your first task as a new couple should be the establishing of a budget. This is simply a list of your expenses and revenues. It contains a plan for saving, spending, giving and investing. It should be grounded in your financial reality, and is a game plan to tell your money where to go.

Creating a budget should be a team effort, with both partners participating in the process. As you work on your budget, take particular note of your income to debt ratio. Are you finding that after bills are paid you have very little left for savings, or the creation of an emergency fund? Do you find that you put other expenses ahead of paying your tithes or donating to the work of God's kingdom?

How does your budget stack up against the recommended percentages by financial experts

Category	You	Recommended
Charitable Gifts		10-15%
Savings		7-10%
Housings/ Mortgage		28-35%
Utilities		5-10%
Food		8-15%
Transportation		10-15%

Financial problems can put a lot of stress on a new marriage. However, financial problems in a marriage can often be a sign of other problems in the relationship. Money can be the tool that couples use to play out their disappointments, resentment, and neglect.

DEBT

We are a society that has become accustomed to debt. You and your mate may feel pressured to buy things you can't afford to impress others. As couples create this lavish lifestyle of living beyond their resources, they give little regard to their mounting debt, but in the end, the marriage will suffer. The both of you should spend time evaluating your finances and spending habits.

o Yes   Is an increasing percentage of your income
o No   going towards paying down debts?

o Yes   Is your saving cushion inadequate or
o No   nonexistent?

o Yes   Are you near or at the limit of your lines of
o No   credit?

o Yes   Can you only make the minimum payments
o No   on your revolving charge accounts?

o Yes   Are you often late with bill payments?
o No

o Yes   Are you paying bills with money earmarked
o No   for something else?

o Yes   Are you using credit to pay for items you used o No   to buy with
cash

o Yes   If you lost your job, would you be under
o No   immediate financial strain?

o Yes   Are you unsure about how much you owe?
o No

➡️ A yes to two of the above questions is an indicator that you should make debt payoff a priority.

Money and Priorities:

You and your mate may not be able to achieve every financial goal, or support all your needs and wants unless you have an unlimited money resource. That's why it's important to set your goals clearly and have an understanding of what's important to each other. When your efforts are concentrated, you have a better chance of achieving what matters most.

> Read the list below and use this scale to categorize how important each item is to you. Place the appropriate number on the line next to the item. As an example: (1) means its very important to you, while a (4) means it's not important.
>
> 1-Very Important   2- Important   3- Somewhat important   4- Not important

a) _____ Buying clothing from consignment shop
b) _____ Paying your mortgage/ rent on time
c) _____ Ensuring vehicles receive proper maintenance
d) _____ Taking vacations on a regular basis
e) _____ Buying the latest electronics
f) _____ Eating out on a regular basis
g) _____ Regular trips to the beauty salon/or barbershop
h) _____ Paying tithes consistently
i) _____ Driving a brand new car

j)   _____ Paying utility bills on time

k)   _____ Wearing name brand clothes

l)   _____ Paying down debt

m)   _____ Seeing the latest movies, attending plays,   Broadway shows
and concerts

n)   _____ Shopping for bargains

o)   _____ Having an emergency fund

A lot of money issues can be better managed by having a good understanding of your partner's history and concepts related to money. The two of you should spend time answering the questions below and sharing your responses.

QUESTIONS FOR YOU:

1. Who handled the money in your household? (Wrote checks, paid bills, etc.)

_____

_____

2. What are your outstanding debts?

_____

_____

3. Have you filed bankruptcy in the past? If so; explain:

_____

_____

4. What are your current assets?

_____

_____

5. Do you prefer to save or spend?

_____

_____

6. Would you like joint or separate accounts?

_____

_____

7. What are your financial goals?

_____

_____

8. Do you currently use a budget?

_____

_____

9. Is living debt-free important to you?

_____

_____

10. Who do you think should handle the finances (pay bills, handle savings, etc.) after you are married?

_____

_____

11. What is your current FICO credit score?

_____

_____

12. How have you used credit in the past?

_____

_____

13. In the household you grew up, was money saved for a rainy day?

_____

_____

14. In your family, was money spent only on necessities?

_____

_____

15. Was your family always in debt?

_____

_____

16. Was money used freely in your family for entertainment?

_____

_____

17. What money memories do you recall from your family?

_____

_____

18. Do you feel you have an obligation to God in regards to how you spend money?

_____

_____

19. Do you believe in tithing?

_____

_____

20. Do you look at any success you have as a blessing from God?

_____

_____

GOD IS OWNER

The Bible clearly states that God is sole owner of everything. "The earth is the Lord's, and all it Contains" (Psalm 24:1).

Biblical Wisdom:

(Take time to discuss the concepts below)
What is your interpretation of each?
How will you incorporate them into your marriage?

- We are overseers of God's property- God requires us to be good stewards over what he gives.

- God is your source- your place of employment or your business is merely the channel God uses to supply your needs. So your trust and hope has to always be grounded in God alone.

- Matthew 6:24 tells us we cannot serve God and money. For you will love the one and hate the other. We are not to serve money or seek things. But we must seek to do the will of God and he will take care of our needs.

- "The love of money is the root of all kinds of evil" (1 Timothy 6:10) make sure your love for money does not cause your priorities to be misplaced.

- "For which of you, intending to build a tower, does not sit down first and count the cost, whether he has enough to finish it." (Luke 14:28). Proper financial planning in a Marriage can prevent accruing debt, and ensure funds are available for a rainy day.

- Financial Infidelity- Secretly spending money, hiding purchases from your spouse, or putting money in secret accounts is a behavior known as "financial infidelity". This is a very dishonest act in marriages and will eventually cause issues. When this behavior is present in a marriage it prevents the foundation of trust.

- Jesus tells a story of a master who entrusted three of his servants with a portion of his money while he was away. When he returned, he found two of his servants had managed his money well. He praised them and gave them more. However, the third servant was careless with his master's money, so his master took what he had given him and gave it to the other servants. (Mathew 25:14-30).

Adjust Your Money Behavior:

In the first column below, wrtie things that are essential to your life, health, job and faith. In the second Column, write down things that you spend money on that isn't essential to the well-being of your life.

Essential   Non-Essential

_____   _____

_____   _____

_____   _____

_____   _____

_____   _____

_____   _____

_____   _____

_____   _____

Look at the first column and ask: "What can I do to reduce the spending of these items?" Write the answer down for each expense.

Look at the second column and decide when you will eliminate these from your spending since they are not essential.

Comparison or Contentment:

Comparison-

1. Comparison is based on the need for approval.
2. When you compare your financial status to others, nothing will ever be good enough.
3. A marriage invested in appearances and possession is an empty marriage.

4. How can you be freed from comparison?

_____

_____

_____

_____

5. Do you feel comparisons can lead to financial trouble?

_____

_____

_____

_____

6. What does Galatians 6:4 say about comparison?

_____

_____

_____

_____

Contentment-

(The Bible teaches to be content no matter our circumstances) True contentment means to:

1. Have no anxiety or care
2. Tell God your needs
3. Be thankful for what you have

•   Why is true contentment important? (read Philippians 4:11-13)

_____

_____

_____

_____

•   What does Hebrews 13:5 say about contentment?

_____

_____

_____

_____

How much is Enough

Unless you settle the question of how much is enough, you will never be satisfied with your lifestyle. There are always more ways to spend money. Even if you suddenly found yourself with millions, you could convince yourself that it isn't enough.

What is Compulsive Spending/Shopping?

Compulsive Spending/Shopping- Is described as a pattern of chronic, repetitive purchasing that becomes difficult to stop. It is a destructive addiction that can turn to financial disaster.

Look at the list below and circle "yes" to all that apply to your spending habits:

◊   Yes   Shop or spend money as a result of being
                    disappointed, angry, or scared

◊   Yes   Shopping/spending habits causing emotional
                    distress or chaos in one's life

◊   Yes   Having arguments with others regarding
                    shopping or spending habits

◊   Yes   Feel lost without credit cards o Yes Buying
                    items on credit that would not be bought with
                    cash

◊   Yes   Spending money causes a rush of euphoria
                    and anxiety at the same time

◊   Yes   Spending or shopping feels like a reckless or
                    forbidden act

◊   Yes   Lying to others about what was bought and
                    how much was spent

◊   Yes   Thinking excessively about money

◊ Yes   Spending a lot of time juggling accounts and
         bills

According to the Illinois Institute for Addiction Recovery, four or more of the above money habits indicates a problem with shopping or spending:

Steps to Take:

I. Avoid visiting stores or websites unless you really need something- Don't put yourself in a situation where you might be tempted to spend.
II. Employ "delay spending rule" if you're going to buy something, give yourself at least 72 hours to think about it. 30 days on big ticket items.
III. Ask questions- before you check out ask yourself do I really need this?
IV. Create a want list- if you cannot afford to pay cash for the item, add it to the want list, and walk away. As you pay down debt and money becomes available you can pick items off your want list and pay cash for them.
V. Only Carry Cash- If you're a compulsive spender, your goal is to break the spending habit. You have to begin to make the connection between buying something and actually spending money. Credit cards and sometimes checks and debit cards, can make this connection fuzzy. Use cash.
VI. Seek Help- If you are unable to get your spending under control, seek help.

More Detail Discussion:

How will we share financial responsibilities?

There are several responsibilities when it comes to household finances: (1) earning (2) budgeting (3) saving and spending (4) administrative (paying bills, etc.) Talk about how you will split responsibilities, and who will tackle what based on strengths and skills.

How will we talk about money?

Unfortunately, many people lie to their spouse about spending. Make a pact not to be one of those couples. Make a plan and document how you are going to talk about money. Discuss how often you will sit down and do a check-in. Will it be once a week, twice a month, etc. Discuss how you will handle if one has bad news. What are your areas of sensitivity, and how should they be approached (i.e. don't talk to me about bills after work when I'm stressed)? Set some ground rules to make talking about money easier.

Where do we want to be in 5 or 10 years?

Talk about and set specific money goals together. A "comfortable lifestyle" might mean a $200,000 household income to one person, and $1 million to another. Discuss what kind of lifestyle you want, how many homes you want, how often you want to go on vacation, and then, this is important: Crunch the numbers- will you be able to afford this? If not, you may have to adjust either your income, or your expectations.

How much do we have, and where is it?

It's surprising how many people don't know their net worth, but it's an important number to start with. Sit down and get a global picture of each other's assets. See where you stand, and where the money is located (in stocks, 401k, real estate, car, etc.) it's good to get a complete picture as a starting point to build from.

What's your credit score?

Your credit score is your "financial responsibility" number- and it impacts everything from your ability to open a line of credit, to your mortgage interest rate. The "why" is as important as the "what" when it comes to conversations about credit scores. If one has bad credit, ask them why. Were they unable to make payments because they overspent on that vacation, or got laid off? And don't just take your partners word for it. Take a few moments to check your scores together.

Do we want children, and if so, who will work?

Children are expensive. Not only should you discuss the work situation- will one work and one stay home? How will you share income and child-rearing responsibilities? When will we start trying to have children, and how many? Although, only God can predict the future 100 percent, having conversations early on (i.e. if you plan to work and not have one as a stay at home parent) will prevent misunderstanding later.

<u>Debt Reduction Tips:</u>

1. Make a budget and list all your monthly bills and necessities. Stay within your budget guidelines.

2. Learn to use cash instead of credit cards.

3. Eliminate your unnecessary expenses, such as expensive meals out.

4. Evaluate your housing situation. Your housing cost should be no more than 35% of your household income, this includes mortgage payments, property tax, and home-owner's insurance.

5. Stop borrowing money and cut up your credit cards.

6. Shop around to find deals, bargains, and savings. You can often save a lot by taking the time to shop around and compare prices.

7. Establishing an emergency fund will help you better manage unexpected expenses.

8. Use the snowball method to pay down debt.

9. Have regular meetings about debt.

10. Pay more than the minimum payment.

Budget- Identifying Spending Categories:

What spending categories should you include in your budget? Below are basic categories that are helpful to include in your budget, they cover most of the major spending categories most people encounter each month:

*   Giving: Tithing to your church or giving to nonprofit organizations

*   House: Electricity and utilities, TV, mortgage, and other expenses for your home

*   Food: Grocery store shopping

*   Auto: auto insurance, gasoline, oil changes, car payments

*   Insurance: Life, medical, dental

*   Debt: Credit card, loans

- Entertainment: Dining out, movies, vacations

- Clothing: Seasonal clothing needs

- Savings: emergency fund, car etc.

- Medical: Over the counter medications, doctors co-pays

- Miscellaneous: Anything that doesn't fit into another category

- Investments: Investments outside of 401k which may include IRA, Roth IRA, etc.

- School/Childcare- Pre-school and other school related expenses

The first budget the two of you make together will require some educated guessing. Once you've tracked spending according to your budget categories for a few months, you can make changes where you may have estimated too high or too low. In doing so, your budget will more accurately reflect actual spending behavior.

Detailed Budget Example:

Gross Monthly Income: _____
Salary: _____
Interest: _____
Dividends: _____
Other income: _____
Less:
Giving: _____
Taxes (Fed, State, FICA) _____
Net Spending Income: _____

Living Expenses:
1. Housing

Mortgage or Rent: _____
Insurance: _____
Property Taxes: _____
Electricity: _____

Heating/Gas: _____

Water: _____

Garbage Service: _____

Telephone: _____

Maintenance: _____

Cleaning & Supplies: _____

Other: _____

2. **Food:** _____
3. **Transportation:** _____

Payments: _____
Gas & Oil: _____
Insurance: _____
Maint/Repair-Replace: _____
Other: _____

4. **Insurance**:

Life: _____
Medical: _____
Dental: _____
Other: _____

5. **Debts**: _____
   (Except auto & house payments)

6. **Entertainment/Recreation:**

Babysitters: _____
Vacation: _____

Pets: _____

Other: _____

7. Clothing: _____

8. Savings: _____

9. Medical Expenses: _____

Doctor: _____

Prescriptions: _____

Other: _____

10.   Miscellaneous:

Toiletries: _____

Laundry/Cleaning: _____

Allowances: _____

Subscriptions: _____

Birthdays/Anniversaries: _____

Weddings/Showers: _____

Graduations: _____

Christmas Presents: _____

Postage: _____

Accounting/Legal: _____

Education: _____

Other: _____

11. School/Child Care:

Tuition: _____

Day Care: _____

Other: _____

12. Investments: _____

Total Living Expense: _____

Net Spendable Income: _____

Less Total Living Expenses: _____

Surplus or Deficit: _____

COUPLES TESTIMONY

Finances

Married 21 Years:

How do you handle finances in your marriage?

Prior to getting married, we had many conversations about money and we found that we had some different opinions about how we should set up our accounts. My idea (Rebecca) was to put all funds together and then set up a joint saving and checking account from that pool of money. My idea (Larry) was to allocate ample funds to be deposited into the joint checking account and savings account and then each would then use funds that were left for personal accounts as each choose. After many discussions we decided to follow the plan of each of us, allocating equal amounts to be deposited into joint checking and saving accounts. **We decided that it was very important for each of us to have some freedom in using some of the funds as we choose.**

Do you operate from a budget?

We do operate from a budget. We calculate what amount of money is necessary to take care of monthly and yearly expenses and then we allocate funds above that amount to be deposited into the joint checking account. The joint checking account is utilized to pay all household accounts including house insurance, property taxes, auto insurance, auto registration, car repairs etc. It is also used for our vacation expenses. We decided each of us would designate equal amounts of funds each pay period for the two joint accounts.

What financial challenges do you think couples face in today's society?

It is a challenge to ever be mindful that efforts must be put forth constantly to obtain agreement about finances. This may require reevaluating the financial plan and reviewing financial decisions of the past. One major challenge is the lack of understanding that each person in a marriage need to have money they can boss around and use as they choose. When there is no freedom for that then there will be a lording over one another in regard to how money is spent for personal satisfaction.

No adult wants to always have to get permission to spend money for something that is important to them. **If funds are available for each to use as they choose there will be honesty and transparency in respect to finances.** To do this may be a challenge in these difficult economic times. But it is important even if the funds are meager, there should be some money when possible that each can use as they choose.

It is also a challenge to stay in balance according to God's plan. That is being faithful in our tithing and offering. **We believe God's balance plan is Give, Spend, Save.** Certainly being faithful to God is the challenge that couples face in today's tough economic times. God is a God that understands that and His challenge is to prove Him.
What financial advice would you give engaged and married couples?

First and foremost to both engaged and married couples. Be honest with God in returning a faithful tithe and offering. The rule; give, spend and save is profitable for all in whatever status of life.
Engaged Couples:

The advice we would give engaged couples is take time to understand each other's attitude toward money, which includes spending habits. Have many discussions about what each other think about the financial plan they will establish together. **While money concerns may not seem to be that important in the dating stage, it is critical for a happy marriage.** It is also important to be transparent about existing debt. It can be devastating to a couple beginning marriage when there are existing debts to be dealt with. If there are debts develop a plan to eliminate them prior to marriage if possible.

Through the conversations we had we created a plan that worked for us and has worked for us without any problems at all for over 21 years. And when we say without any problems we mean we have never had any argument or disagreement about finances ever in our marriage. We attribute that to two realities; 1) each of us had some freedom with funds that were ours to use as we choose, 2) we have similar ideas about money.

We decided to open a joint account prior to getting married. That may be a good idea for engaged couples to actually test a part of their financial plan to see how it will work prior to marriage. **A critical consideration is that if a financial attitude is identified that creates a problem it must be dealt with and resolved prior to marriage.** Do not expect that marriage will change that issue, as a matter of fact, the problem will possibly get worse.

Married couples

The advice we would offer those that are already married is to understand money have been given to us by a loving God, and that it is to be used for our temporal comfort and happiness. And that everyone needs to have some money to use as they choose. **Some funds should be allocated to each with the freedom extended to use as they choose**. How they spend that money does not have to make sense to the other partner. (Leaving each person to answer only to God.)

You should keep an open dialogue regarding the financial plan, reviewing and evaluating frequently. And working the plan together so that each has an understanding of the plan and how the funds are spent, what funds are saved, and what funds are set aside for emergencies. **Make every decision for major purchases an occasion for discussion and evaluation so that the burden of financial woes will be minimized.**

Larry & Rebecca

FICO SCORES

Tony and Katava
Married 1 Year

What Is a FICO Score?

A FICO score is a credit score created by the Fair Isaac Corporation (FICO).1 Lenders use borrowers' FICO scores along with other details on borrowers' credit reports to assess credit risk and determined whether to extend credit. FICO scores take into account data in five areas to determined creditworthiness: payment history, current level of indebtedmness, types of credit used, length of credit history, and new credit accounts.

KEY TAKEAWAYS
- FICO credit scores are a method of quantifying and evaluating an individual's creditworthiness

- Scores range from 300 to 850, with scores in the 670 to 739 range considered to be "good" credit history

- The FICO scoring methodology is updated from time to time, with the most recent version now being FICO Score 10- Suite, which was announced on Jan, 23 2020

UNDERSTANDING FICO SCORES

Fico is a major analytics software company that provides products and services to both businesses and consumers. The company is best known for producing the most widely used consumer credit scores that financial institutions use in deciding whether to ledn money or issue credit.

To determine creditworthiness, lenders take a borrower's FICO score into account, but they also consider other details, such as income, how long the borrower has been at their job, and the type of credit requested.

FICO scores are used in more than 90% of the credit decisions made in the U.S. Although borrowers can explain negative items in their credit report, the fact remains that having a low FICO score is a deal breaker with numerous lenders. Many lenders maintain hard-and-fast FICO minimums for approval, particularly in the mortgage industry. One point below this threshold results in a denial. Therefore, a strong argument exists that borrowers should prioritize FICO above all bureaus when trying to build or improve credit.

The major factors used ina FICO score are:

Payment history (35%)
Payment history refers to whether an individual pays their credit accounts on time. Credit reports show the payments submitte for each line of credit, and the reports detail bankruptcy or collection items along with any late or mised payments.

Accounts owed (30%)
Accounts owed refers to the amount of money an individual owes. Having a lot of debt does not necessarily equate to low credit scores. Rather, FICO considered the ratio of money owed to the amount of credit available. To illustrate, an individual who owes $10,000 but has all of their lines of credit fully extended and all of their credit cares maxed out may have a lower credit score than an individual who owes $100,000 but is not close to the limit on any of their accounts.

Length of Credit History (15%)
As a general rule of thumb, the longer an individual has had credit, the better their score. However, with favorable scores in the other categories, even someone with a short credit history can have a good score. FICO scores take into account how long the oldest account has been open, the age of the newest account, and the overall average.

Credit mix (10%)
Credit mix is the variety of accounts. To obtain high credit scores, individuals need a strong mix of retail accounts; credit cards; installment loans, such as signature loans or vehicle loans; and mortgages.

New Credit (10%)
New Credit refers to recently opened accounts. If a borrower has opened a bunch of new accounts in a short period of time, that indicates risk and lowers their score.

FICO SCORE

1. When did you first hear about the Fico Score?

_____

_____

_____

_____

2. At what age did you purchase your first credit/charge card?

_____

_____

_____

_____

3. Do you currently use credit cards?

_____

_____

_____

_____

4. How do you feel about credit cards?

_____

_____

_____

_____

5. Do you know your credit score?

_____

_____

_____

_____

6. Do you know your partner's credit score?

_____

_____

_____

_____

** I strongly recommend you show your credit score information to your partner. Credit scores will play a tremendous role in your marriage as you build together.

DOMESTIC DUTIES

HOUSEHOLD CHORES:

A common problem in marriage is often centered on who is responsible for doing the household chores. The traditional division of labor included the man working full-time outside the home and the woman taking care of the house. But now, many women work outside the home. It can be tough when both people are working to get things done around the house

- Do you like to clean house

_____

_____

_____

_____

- Are there certain household habits that drive you crazy? (Like; dirty dishes in sink? etc.)

_____

_____

_____

_____

- How neat are you compared to your mate?

_____

_____

_____

_____

Balance the Load:

To get everyone on the same page and prevent confusion and unfair workloads, the two of you should work together to identify the tasks that need to be accomplished, and who will complete them. While creating your list, take into account how much each of you works outside the home. If one of you are working 20 hours a week and the other is working a full time job, it would be reasonable to expect that the one working less would do more of the housework. There may be other things that need to be accounted for also, like one partner going to school, or one taking care of the children.

To help you get started with this task, we have created a basic chore chart. You and your partner should fill this out together.

CHORE CHART:

Listed below are a number of household chores that will need to be handled. You and your partner should decide together who will do each task. Also, feel free to add any tasks that may be missing from this list.

Task	You	Your Spouse	Both
Yard Work	O	O	O
Car Maintenance	O	O	O
House Maintenance	O	O	O
Laundry	O	O	O
Making the bed	O	O	O
Doing the dishes	O	O	O
Cleaning	O	O	O
Cooking & Baking	O	O	O
Taking out trash	O	O	O
Grocery Shopping	O	O	O
Decorating	O	O	O

For The Sake of Us

Task	You	Your Spouse	Both
Ironing	O	O	O
Vacuuming	O	O	O
Mop Floors	O	O	O
Shampoo Carpet	O	O	O

GENDER DIFFERENCES

Jon and Dericka
Married 4 Months

MALE/FEMALE DIFFERENCES

Often times when couples first meet, it's the differences that attract them to each other. But after marriage, those same differences can become a source of marital tension. In fact, a lot of time and energy can be spent trying to change each other rather than valuing the ways God created him or her differently.

It's important to spend some time understanding how God has created the male and female differently. This should enhance your appreciation for your mate, and hopefully provide ideas to better connect your two worlds. It's also important to understand that while we are different as individuals, and there are gender differences, we still have more in common than what separates us.

There has been a lot of research done on this topic, we present some of the common gender differences below:

Gender Differences

Male	Female

Communication

Male	Female
Conversation focus on facts	Female conversation emphasize feelings behind facts.
Solve problems best by thinking of one issue at a time, normally on their own.	Talk through problems with someone else to process their thoughts.
Speak directly and use words literally.	Tend to speak indirectly
Approach situations with desire to take action	Approach situations to talk about how they feel about it
Messages heard transformed into information	Messages heard transformed into emotions.

Process Information

High ability to compartmentalize	Low ability to compartmentalize
Brain highly systematic	Brain highly empathetic
Low ability to multitask	High ability to multitask
Aggressive response to risk	Cautions response to risk

EMOTIONAL

Not very sensitive	Tend to be very sensitive
Hard to express feelings through the use of language	Emphasis on using language or action to express feelings
Use language of the head	Use language of the heart
Difficulty in displaying physical affection	More emphasis on physical affection
Solution orientated	Messages heard transformed into emotions. Need feelings understood and accepted
Analytical and rational	Emotional and temperamental

SEX

Stimulaed by sight	Stimulated by touch and romantic words
Intensely physical experience	Intensely emotional experience
Initiate sex at any time	Initiate sex less frequently
Display of desire	Display of affection
No preparation needed	Need tenderness, kind words to prepare

Other Differences:

Further research reveals the bundle of nerves in the brain that connects emotion and cognition in females is up to 20% larger than in males. This gives females better decision making and sensory processing skills. All learning must connect emotion and cognition. Because of this difference in size, females rely heavily on verbal communication; males tend to rely heavily on nonverbal communication and are less likely to verbalize feelings.

Females are dominated by estrogen and progesterone, males by testosterone. These hormones are contrasting in their effects. Progesterone, for instance, is a female growth hormone and also the bonding hormone. Testosterone is the male growth hormone and also the sex-drive and aggression hormone.

Women are more likely to talk to other women when they have a problem or need to make a decision. Men keep their problems to themselves and don't see the point in sharing personal issues.

Women are more relationship oriented, and look for commonalities and ways to connect with other women. Men tend to relate to other men from a status and dominance standpoint. Women focus on building rapport by sharing experiences and asking questions. Men like to tell and give information rather than ask questions.

Questions for you:

1. Have you noticed any gender differences in your relationship?

_____
_____
_____
_____

2. Do any of the gender differences from the above list surprise you?

_____
_____
_____
_____

For The Sake of Us

3. What is your game plan to deal with gender differences?

_____

_____

_____

_____

4. What do you think will be the greatest gender challenge in your marriage?

_____

_____

_____

_____

5. What do you think your partner would list as the greatest gender challenge?

_____

_____

_____

_____

6. Explain the impact for a couple that does not deal with differences effectively?

_____

_____

_____

_____

7. Have you observed gender related issues in other marriages?

_____

_____

_____

_____

8. How can gender differences be used to enhance a marriage?

_____

_____

_____

_____

9. List some of the differences you appreciate about your mate?

_____

_____

_____

_____

10. How will you celebrate the similarities in your marriage?

_____

_____

_____

_____

INTIMACY

Nancy and Michael
Married 32 Years

INTIMACY

There is no other relationship that yields the depth of intimacy like marriage does. Within this intimate relationship, partners are given the opportunity to know and be known in a way that is not possible outside of the martial union. This husband and wife relationship unifies mind, body, and spirit into one.

- What does intimacy mean to you?

_____

_____

_____

_____

Types of Intimacy:

Intimacy is more than the sex act. Although sexual encounters are part of the intimacy process, it involves much more. An intimate marriage should include physical, emotional, intellectual, social and spiritual intimacy.

Physical - Sexual and non-sexual touch and affection.

Emotional - When emotional intimacy is present, you can share personal feelings without being judged, there is an environment of trust, there is also an overall feeling of being safe and secure with each other.

Intellectual - is the connection of your minds and being able to have deep and intimate conversations with each other.
Social - Is engaging in projects. Sharing mutual activities together and spending time with each other.

Spiritual - This is the most important intimacy, because it impacts all others. Through Spiritual Intimacy, couples connect with each other by seeking God's leadership in their marriage. They come together in prayer to seek the lord and the things of His kingdom for their lives and family. They share the same Spiritual values and principles. Through this intimacy, closeness happens that can only be orchestrated by God.

Intimacy Check-in

Unconditional love in a marriage creates an environment where husband and wife can be vulnerable and transparent. This openness produces profound intimacy and fulfills one our greatest needs, which is to be truly known. Let's take time to do an intimacy check-in to see how well you and your partner are progressing in the various types of intimacy.

For the next several questions, please choose a number from 1-10 and write it next to each statement to indicate how much you agree with that statement:

1	2	3	4	5	6	7	8	9	10
Disagree		Somewhat Disagree		Somewhat agree		Agree		Strongly Agree	

_____ I pray regularly for my partner-

_____ My partner and I pray together on a regular basis-

_____ My partner and I read and study the bible together-

_____ I feel comfortable talking to my partner about God-

_____ I participate in my partner's interests and hobbies-

_____ My partner support me in my personal interests-

_____ I can express my opinion when my partner may disagree-

_____ My partner and I have conversations about a variety of topics-

_____ I feel safe being vulnerable with my partner-

_____ My partner says "I love you" to me often-

_____ My partner and I spend quality time together often-

_____ I enjoy spending time in conversation with my partner-

_____   My partner is my best friend-

_____   My partner remembers the special days in my life-

_____   My partner and I pray together to help resolve our conflict

What's Important?

There are certain activities and actions that can help build marital intimacy, we have listed some below: Use the scale to rate how important these are to you. Also rate how important you think they are to your mate.

1	2	3	4	5
Not Important				**Very Important**

<u>You</u>   <u>Mate</u>

_____   _____   Spending quality time together

_____   _____   Surprise dinner out at your favorite restaurant

_____   _____   Holding hands

_____   _____   Praying together

_____   _____   Hearing "I love you"

_____   _____   Being accepted

_____   _____   Receiving hugs

_____   _____   Being respected

_____   _____   Receiving encouragement

_____   _____   Receiving a love note

_____ 　　　 _____ My mate sharing my hobbies

_____ 　　　 _____ Receiving surprise gifts

_____ 　　　 _____ Having quiet conversations

Now, if you listed more than one item as very important use the space below to rank them in order of importance to you.

_____

_____

_____

_____

Barriers to Intimacy:

Lack of Communication- If meaningful communication is missing, then every area of the relationship will be hampered.

Lack of Trust- When trust is missing from a relationship you cannot build true intimacy.

Lack of Commitment- Commitment is the glue that holds a relationship together and allows intimacy to develop.

Companionship Builds Intimacy:
Look at the paired statements below: Put a check by the one you would choose.

o Night out with Friends
o Night out with Spouse

o Watching favorite TV show
o Talking quietly with spouse

o Attending game of favorite sports team
o Quiet dinner with spouse

Seven components of Intimate Interactions (adapted from L' Abate, 1977) Use the scale below, rate your relationship on each component of intimate interactions

Component of Intimacy	Low					High
1. Seeing the Good: Expressing appreciation, affection, and affirmation	1.	2.	3.	4.	5.	6

Component of Intimacy	Low					High
2. Caring: Concern about the other's welfare, happiness, needs, and feelings in a consistent and dependable way.	1.	2.	3.	4.	5.	6.
3. Protectiveness: Need to protect each other and their relationship	1.	2.	3.	4.	5.	6.

Component of Intimacy	Low					High
4. Enjoyment: Being together and doing things together that are pleasurable	1	2	3	4	5	6
5. Responsibility: Accepting responsibility for one's part in the relationship	1	2	3	4	5	6
6. Sharing Hurt: Sharing feelings of pain or suffering with each other	1	2	3	4	5	6
7. Forgiveness: Achieved through an understanding of the other person's motivation, cherishing the goodwill that pervades the relationship	1	2	3	4	5	6

Growing in Intimacy:

Date Night:

Oftentimes married couples do not think about dating their spouse. They may think this activity is reserved for single people looking for a mate. It might sound silly, why date your spouse?

Date night is a great way to keep your relationship alive and exciting. Dating also create moments in the relationship that will become lasting memories.

- How often would you like you and your mate to have a date night?

_____

_____

_____

_____

- Describe your perfect date?

_____

_____

_____

_____

Connecting with God:

Staying connected to God as a couple will breathe life into your marriage and give a solid foundation for tough times. Make a daily or weekly date with your spouse to seek God together.

- How will you and your mate seek God together?

_____

_____

_____

_____

Celebrating Special Days:

The both of you have special days or events that you consider to be important in your life. An example of a special day could be a birthday or anniversary; a special event could be a promotion at work. Knowing the days and events that your partner considers important, and celebrating those in a special way will enhance your relationship.

• What are special days for you? How would you like them celebrated?

_____

_____

_____

_____

• What are special events for you? How would you like them celebrated?

_____

_____

_____

_____

Just Because:

There are times when you need to do something nice for your spouse "just because". Buy a card, send flowers, or plan a special night out to show your spouse that you are thinking of them.

List some of the special things you will do for your partner after marriage.

_____

_____

_____

_____

Intimacy with God:

The main key to having an intimate relationship with your mate is to strive for an intimate relationship with God. Inside each of us, God has placed a strong desire for intimacy with Him. God made us with this craving for Him; if you want to develop a deep marital intimacy, you must first develop a deep personal intimacy with God. Intimacy with God starts with pursuing Him with our whole heart. King David wrote, "When you said, seek my face, my heart said to you, your face, o Lord I shall seek." (psalms 27:8) God invites us in James 4:8 "to draw near to Him and He will draw near to us."

Because God made us, He intimately knows us better than anyone can. For this reason, He can make us feel known in a way that no one on earth is able; and in this we can experience intimacy in an indescribable way. It is in this environment that we experience true love, grace, and mercy. Through this type of intimacy we find the strength and the power to love our partner unconditionally, and to share our life as an open book.

More Discussions:

History:

- Growing up, who could you rely on to share in your sadness and hurts?

_____

_____

_____

_____

- As a teenager, were you shown approval for the things you accomplished or for who you were?

_____

_____

_____

_____

- Who gave you attention as a youth?

_____

_____

_____

_____

More Questions:

• Describe what makes you feel loved.

_____
_____
_____
_____

• Describe how you show love.

_____
_____
_____
_____

• What is the best way for your partner to develop intimacy with you?

_____
_____
_____
_____

• Has your partner shared their future dreams with you?

_____
_____
_____
_____

• In your opinion, what was your best date? What made it special?

_____
_____
_____
_____

• Have you shared your future dreams with your partner?

_____
_____
_____
_____

- Have you learned to accept the fact that God loves you as you are?

_____
_____
_____
_____

- Have you learned to accept the fact that God loves your mate as they are?

_____
_____
_____
_____

- Do you share your feelings honestly and openly with your mate?

_____
_____
_____
_____

- What are some of the areas preventing closeness in your relationship?

_____
_____
_____
_____

- What areas do you feel your partner has the most difficulty being open?

_____
_____
_____
_____

- What areas do you have the most difficulty being open?

_____
_____
_____
_____

Biblical Wisdom:

Take time to discuss the principles below: What is your interpretation of each? How will you incorporate them into your marriage?

Dear friends, let us love one another, for love comes from God. Everyone who loves has been born of God and knows God. 1 John 4:7

For this reason a man will leave his father and mother and be united to his wife, and they will become one flesh. Genesis 2:24

The man and his wife were both naked, and they felt no shame. Genesis 2:25

So God created man in His own image, in the image of God he created him; male and female he created them. Genesis 1:27

COUPLE TESTIMONY

Intimacy

Married for 22 Years:

Intimacy allows a couple to connect in ways that will create wholeness in the marriage. The physical part allows couples to release built up frustration from everyday living. Emotionally it provides security in the fact that there is someone whom you can confide in and trust with your true feelings. Intellectually, you feel this connection within and you want to make sure that you are not just trying to satisfy yourself but connect with your spouse so that you both can reach the same outcome. When we feel the same connection mentally, the needs of the home and the ministry are taken care of. When knowing each other on a deeper level mentally we sometimes find ourselves completing each other sentences or thoughts.

Socially, it is great to spend time together doing things that we like to do or want to do. But it is also good to spend some time alone or with other friends, who share the same values that you do about love and marriage.

Spiritually there is nothing greater than to be able to spend time in worship with your spouse. It allows you to be connected to God so that you both may hear how he is guiding you in your marriage, family and ministry.

Having busy lives (ministry, family, jobs, and other activities) can sometimes result in frustration and tiredness. Because of this we often lack the energy or the will to connect in any kind of intimacy. There are challenges of where do you draw the line in fulfilling intimacy acts or needs. More than often this effects the physical intimacy. Initiation of intimacy can be a big challenge in the marriage related to who is going to be the one to initiate sex. **We have committed to set aside special times alone with each other, to openly talk about our personal needs and desires. This leads to fulfillment for one another.**

Through prayer, a lot of our challenges have been overcome. It can still be a struggle to put the needs of each other first, but the willingness is stronger than when we were first married. We are determined to allow God restoration in this area.

Be willing to truthfully talk openly about your needs and desires in every area of

intimacy. Never assume that you know everything about what your spouse needs. Continue to pray about satisfying your spouse and checking on where they are in that area.

Michael & Nancy

SEX

Leroy and Naaila
Married 2 Years

SEX

Over the centuries there has been many thoughts and viewpoints related to sex. From the historical thought process that sex is evil and should only be used in marriage for procreation, to our modern day view of have sex whenever you want, with whomever you want.

Both extremes are wrong and fail to fulfill God's intended function of sex. The book of Genesis is a great place to start; to see God's plan for sex within the martial relationship.

God's Plan:

In chapter 2 of Genesis, we see God performing the first marriage and giving Adam and Eve the command to be fruitful and multiply. This is a command for males and females to engage in sexual relations within the confines of marriage. The God idea of sex is not just for procreation, but also for sexual fulfillment. God has given us marriage where we can enjoy physical relations without guilt. (Hebrews 13:4).

• What does the word "sex" mean to you?

_____
_____
_____
_____

The biblical writers affirm the goodness of sexuality as God's gift. The Song of Solomon has explicit erotic imagery and language. Within this book, sex is affirmed as a source of pleasure and shared intimacy between husband and wife.

• Do you see sex as a gift from God? Explain?

_____
_____
_____
_____

Sexual activity as presented in the bible is only honored within the context of the marital covenant. As a result of this covenant the man and woman may be naked, and not ashamed. The bible confirms sexual relations are limited to this covenant relationship. All forms of sexual activity outside the marriage covenant are condemned.

• Why do you think God reserves sex for the marriage relationship only?

_____
_____
_____
_____

• Do you think sex outside of marriage is wrong?

_____
_____
_____
_____

• Can you think of ways where sex outside of marriage can cause damage?

_____
_____
_____
_____

Human sexuality and sexual passions were addressed openly in the bible. Paul admonished those who have not been given the gift of celibacy to marry, rather than allow their passions to turn into sinful lust. (1 Corinthians 7:9)

The husband and wife are ordered to offer their bodies to each other, and fulfill their sexual obligations. The only exception was for a short period for fasting and prayer. (1 Corinthians 7:3-5)

• Will you feel comfortable after marriage discussing your sexual likes and dislikes with your partner?

_____
_____
_____
_____

- What are your sexual expectations after marriage?

_____

_____

_____

_____

Right Perspective:

Sexuality is part of our embodied existence. As sexual creatures, we are called to honor God with our bodies. Within the context of the marital covenant, the husband and wife are free to express love for each other, experience pleasure, and join in the procreative act of sexual union. This is pleasing to God, and not to be a source of shame.

- What are your fears concerning sex after you are married?

_____

_____

_____

_____

- Do you feel comfortable talking to God about your sexual issues?

_____

_____

_____

_____

- How can you honor God with your body?

_____

_____

_____

_____

Temptation:

Because of our sex-saturated culture, we are faced with additional pressure when it comes to fighting sexual temptation. The battle now is harder than it's ever been. As a married couple, one or both of you may be faced with temptation. You must know that God requires you to actively fight sexual temptation. He says to flee immorality (1 Corinthians 6:18). In fact, God says to offer not even a hint of sexual immorality

(Ephesians 5:3). Because of the society in which we live, we now have to include other elements in the temptation bucket, such as virtual sex, phone sex with strangers, sexual conversations in chat rooms, and porn sites. All of these are a violation of God's intention. Just because you are not physically touching another person's body doesn't mean it's not sin, Jesus said sexual sin happens in the mind first. (Matthew 5:28)

Boundaries:

A good way to win over sexual temptation is to establish good boundaries:

- Boundaries are established lines that indicate how far you will go
- Boundaries help us decide when enough is enough
- Boundaries determine our behavior in given situations
- Boundaries let us know when to say yes, and when to say no

An example of a boundary could be "not to visit the opposite sex at home alone". How have you handled temptation in the past?

_____

_____

_____

_____

- What does God mean when He says to flee immorality?

_____

_____

_____

_____

- What boundaries will you put in place to protect your marriage from temptation?

_____

_____

_____

_____

Insecurities:

Another thing that can impact the relationship and your sexual experience is personal insecurities. If you find in the relationship that you are having feelings of insecurities of any kind, you should talk to your partner immediately about your feelings. Insecurities can be a devastating tool, often times the person feels that they are not good enough, or do not measure up in some area. Most people suffer from insecurity at some time, but prolonged insecurity is not healthy.

In order to help you get this conversation started with your mate, we have listed some insecurities below: Please check the ones that apply to you. We have also left additional space for you to list any other insecurity that is not on the list below.

- o   I don't like the way my body look so I have issues with certain parts of my body
- o   I worry I will not perform well sexually
- o   I am unhappy with my weight-
- o   I worry my mate will want someone else
- o   I don't feel very attractive
- o   I have issues being seen naked
- o   I wish I was a different height
- o   I worry my mate will not find me sexually desirable-

_____

_____

_____

_____

More Discussions:

History:
- How did you learn about sex?

_____

_____

_____

_____

- Was sex discussed openly in your family?

_____

_____

_____

_____

- Did you date as a teenager?

  _____
  _____
  _____
  _____

- Growing up, were there any issues of infidelity in your household?

  _____
  _____
  _____
  _____

- Have you been sexually abused before? Have you discussed this with your partner?

  _____
  _____
  _____
  _____

- Have you ever been involved in an adulterous affair?

  _____
  _____
  _____
  _____

- Have you discussed in detail your sexual past with your mate?

  _____
  _____
  _____
  _____

- How do you view sex now compared to when you were a teenager?

  _____
  _____
  _____
  _____

- What events from the past have done the most to shape your views on sex?

_____

_____

_____

_____

- Are there any sexual sins that you need to ask for God's forgiveness?

_____

_____

_____

_____

More Questions:

- Do you look at your partner as a sexual object?

_____

_____

_____

_____

- Do you see the sexual act as a fulfillment of your love for your mate?

_____

_____

_____

_____

- Who should initiate love making?

_____

_____

_____

_____

- How often do you think about sex?

_____

- How often do you want to make love?

_____

- Are there any places you feel uncomfortable being touched?

_____

- When being sexual, do you put the emphasis on sex as a loving experience or sex as a performance?

_____

- Do you feel that the sexual act should be about focusing on your partner's satisfaction or on your own satisfaction?

_____

- Do you have any sexual problems that you don't know how to solve?

_____

- Do you feel you and your partner will be able to discuss openly your sexual feelings and responses?

_____
_____
_____
_____

- How important will sex be in your marriage?

_____
_____
_____
_____

- Do you feel you and your partner have a sound and healthy attitude about sex?

_____
_____
_____
_____

- Are there any sexual acts that make you feel uncomfortable, or to be considered immoral?

_____
_____
_____
_____

- How will you communicate your sexual needs to your partner?

_____
_____
_____
_____

- Do you feel you have a good understanding of your partner's sexual past?

_____
_____
_____
_____

Biblical Wisdom:

Take time to discuss the principles below:
What is your interpretation of each?
How will you incorporate them into your marriage?

It is God's will that you should be sanctified, that you should avoid sexual immorality, that each of you should learn to control his own body in a way that is holy and honorable, not in passionate lust like the heathen, who do not know God, 1 Thessalonians 4:3-5

May your fountain be blessed, and may you rejoice in the wife of your youth. A loving doe, a graceful deer– may her breasts satisfy you always, may you ever be captivated by her love. Proverbs 5:18-19

The husband should fulfill his marital duty to his wife, and likewise the wife to her husband. The wife's body does not belong to her alone but also to her husband. In the same way, the husband's body does not belong to him alone but also to his wife. Do not deprive each other except by mutual consent and for a time, so that you may devote yourselves to prayer. Then come together again so that Satan will not tempt you because of your lack of self-control.
1 Corinthians 7:3-5

Flee from sexual immorality. All other sins a man commits are outside his body, but he who sins sexually sins against his own body. 1 Corinthians 6:18

Do you not know that your body is a temple of the holy Spirit, who is in you, whom you have received from God? You are not your own, you were bought at a price. Therefore honor God with your body. 1 Corinthians 6:19-20

THE FORMER MARRIAGE

THE FORMER MARRIAGE:

Holding on to romantic attachments from a previous mate can cause major issues in a new relationship. Also, not learning from the mistakes that caused a previous marriage to fail could bring those same mistakes to the current relationship. Chances are both ex-partners hold some responsibility for the failed marriage. You may have tried your best to save the previous marriage, but playing the blame game does not help your current relationship.

The purpose of this exercise is to help you step back and reflect on your previous marriage, learn from the mistakes, and make sure you have resolved all romantic attractions. This new marriage is a chance to do it better and get it right. It is a chance for you to give your best efforts to your new partner. You must make sure that you have resolved all the issues from the previous marriage, so that you can put it behind you and focus on the new marriage.

As you work through the questions below: it's important to be open and honest and share your answers and emotions with your new partner.

Resolving the Past:

1. How long has it been since your previous marriage ended?

_____

_____

_____

_____

2. How did the divorce make you feel?

_____

_____

_____

_____

3. What did your spouse do that contributed to the breakup of the marriage? Be sure to list specific actions and attitudes.

_____

_____

_____

_____

4. What did you do that contributed to the breakup of the marriage? Be sure to list specific actions and attitudes.

_____

_____

_____

_____

5. Describe how you tried to work through the problems in your previous marriage?

_____

_____

_____

_____

6. What emotions do you have when you see your previous spouse?

_____

_____

_____

_____

7. How did you relate to your previous spouse?

_____

_____

_____

_____

8. How did your previous spouse relate to you?

_____

_____

_____

_____

9. How have your feelings about yourself changed since your previous marriage

_____

_____

_____

_____

10. What are the top issues still lingering from your past marriage?

_____

_____

_____

_____

11. What have you learned about yourself from the past marriage in the following areas:

    -Your needs

_____

_____

_____

_____

    -Your feelings

_____

_____

_____

_____

    -Your goals

_____

_____

_____

_____

    -Your weakness

_____

_____

_____

_____

12. Have you fully forgiven your previous mate?

_____

_____

_____

_____

13. Have you accepted God's forgiveness for your personal failures?

_____

_____

_____

_____

14. What are some ways you will be a better mate because of what you have learned?

_____

_____

_____

_____

15. How is your new partner different from your previous mate?

_____

_____

_____

_____

16. Are there any similarities with your current partner that reminds you of your previous mate?

_____

_____

_____

_____

17. What are the greatest strengths in your new relationship?

_____

_____

_____

_____

18. Do you have any reservations about your new marriage?

_____

_____

_____

_____

19. Finish this sentence- My new marriage will succeed because.

_____

_____

_____

_____

20. What will be the greatest challenge in your new relationship?

_____

_____

_____

_____

www.ingramcontent.com/pod-product-compliance
Lightning Source LLC
Chambersburg PA
CBHW080419030426
42335CB00020B/2503